BONNIE K. HUNTER

String

Strips, Strings & Scrappy Things!

Frenzy

12 MORE
STRING QUILT PROJECTS

C&T PUBLISHING

Text copyright © 2018 by Bonnie K. Hunter
Photography and artwork copyright © 2018 by C&T Publishing, Inc.

Publisher: Amy Marson

Creative Director: Gailen Runge

Acquisitions Editor: Roxane Cerda

Managing Editor: Liz Aneloski

Editor: Kathryn Patterson

Technical Editor: Debbie Rodgers

Cover/Book Designer: April Mostek

Production Coordinator: Zinnia Heinzmann

Production Editor: Alice Mace Nakanishi

Illustrator: Linda Johnson

Photo Assistant: Mai Yong Vang

Photography by Mai Yong Vang of C&T Publishing, Inc.,
unless otherwise noted

Published by C&T Publishing, Inc., P.O. Box 1456, Lafayette, CA 94549

Library of Congress Cataloging-in-Publication Data

Names: Hunter, Bonnie K., author.

Title: String frenzy : 12 more string quilt projects - strips, strings &
scrappy things! / Bonnie K. Hunter.

Description: Lafayette, California : C&T Publishing, Inc., [2018] |
Includes bibliographical references and index.

Identifiers: LCCN 2018009853 | ISBN 9781617457326
(soft cover : alk. paper)

Subjects: LCSH: Patchwork--Patterns. | Quilting--Patterns.

Classification: LCC TT835 .H85366 2018 | DDC 746.46/041--dc23

LC record available at https://lccn.loc.gov/2018009853

Printed in the USA

10 9 8 7 6 5 4 3 2 1

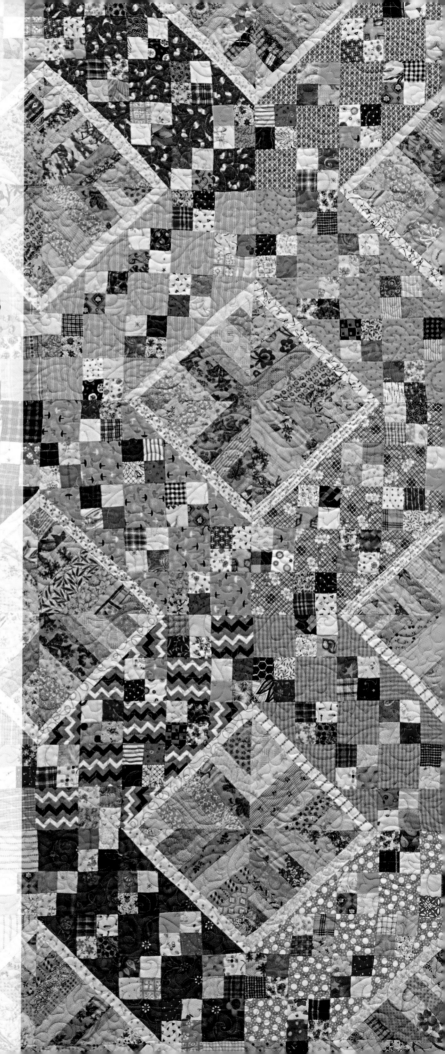

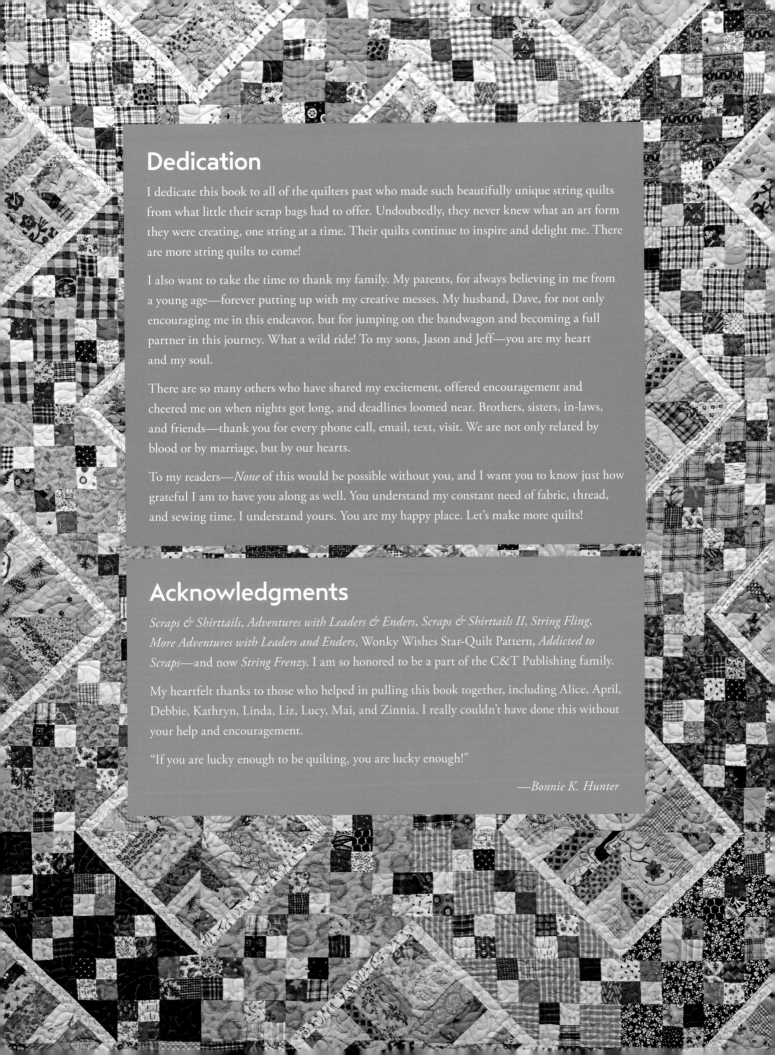

Dedication

I dedicate this book to all of the quilters past who made such beautifully unique string quilts from what little their scrap bags had to offer. Undoubtedly, they never knew what an art form they were creating, one string at a time. Their quilts continue to inspire and delight me. There are more string quilts to come!

I also want to take the time to thank my family. My parents, for always believing in me from a young age—forever putting up with my creative messes. My husband, Dave, for not only encouraging me in this endeavor, but for jumping on the bandwagon and becoming a full partner in this journey. What a wild ride! To my sons, Jason and Jeff—you are my heart and my soul.

There are so many others who have shared my excitement, offered encouragement and cheered me on when nights got long, and deadlines loomed near. Brothers, sisters, in-laws, and friends—thank you for every phone call, email, text, visit. We are not only related by blood or by marriage, but by our hearts.

To my readers—*None* of this would be possible without you, and I want you to know just how grateful I am to have you along as well. You understand my constant need of fabric, thread, and sewing time. I understand yours. You are my happy place. Let's make more quilts!

Acknowledgments

Scraps & Shirttails, *Adventures with Leaders & Enders*, *Scraps & Shirttails II*, *String Fling*, *More Adventures with Leaders and Enders*, Wonky Wishes Star-Quilt Pattern, *Addicted to Scraps*—and now *String Frenzy*. I am so honored to be a part of the C&T Publishing family.

My heartfelt thanks to those who helped in pulling this book together, including Alice, April, Debbie, Kathryn, Linda, Liz, Lucy, Mai, and Zinnia. I really couldn't have done this without your help and encouragement.

"If you are lucky enough to be quilting, you are lucky enough!"

—*Bonnie K. Hunter*

Contents

PROJECTS

FOREWORD

Are you buried in scraps?

Big pieces, small pieces, hunks, chunks, strips, pieces, and parts?

What can you do with all of the small leftovers from other projects that seem too small to save, yet too big to toss away?

I've been in love with fabric for as far back as I can remember and have often asked myself the same thing. And then I ventured into the realm of string piecing and never looked back.

It may seem silly, I know—with yards and yards of "whole" fabric in the stash—to think of stitching all of these small bits back together simply to cut a shape to sew to another shape and then another. But something happened when I did. I was no longer simply following a pattern or design, but creating something unique that danced and dazzled before my eyes.

There is magic in the piecing. Every scrap is full of memories of the project from which it came—every color, texture, and bit of contrast. They might not look like much on their own, these humble little pieces, but together they are a symphony of beauty, each scrap a spot on the timeline of your life as a quilter.

Oh, and did I tell you? String quilts are highly addictive. I dare you to make just one.

The twelve string-based quilts in this book come from my love of antique quilts and many were planted as seeds from blocks I submitted to the *Quiltmaker's* magazine series *100 Blocks by 100 Designers*. Single block submissions demanded to be made into full quilts, and found their way into this book. I hope they whet your appetite for digging into your scraps and creating your own unique, one-of-a-kind string quilts, for each string quilt *is* unique— there are no two alike, ever.

Basic Sewing Guidelines

The patterns for the quilts in this book are based on rotary cutting and machine piecing methods. It is assumed that the reader has a basic knowledge of quilting techniques and processes. The tools needed are those used for basic quilt making: It's necessary to have a sewing machine in good working order (to avoid frustration), but no fancy stitches are required—just a good straight stitch.

That ¼″ Seam Allowance

Accurate cutting and piecing are based on a ¼″ seam allowance. It's important to sew a ¼″ seam with your machine. If you can master this, all your blocks will be the intended size and you'll be able to match points perfectly.

Even if your machine foot has a ¼″ guide on it, it's easy to overshoot a ¼″ seam just by the nature of the guide already being "outside" of the ¼″ foot. Many of us have a habit of running the fabric too hard up against the guide, giving us a seam that is too wide. Do not trust *any* feet with "built-in" guides until you do a seam test!

Do what you have to so your units come out to the appropriate size before going any further. You and your project will be glad you did.

About Project Instructions

Materials lists for scraps are approximate based on cutting all pieces efficiently from 40″-wide strips.

You may use more or less fabric depending on your cutting style, and yardage amounts may vary depending on the number of different fabrics you use and the size of scrap from which you are cutting. Always feel free to add more scraps!

Backing yardage allows for either horizontal or vertical seams, whichever makes the most efficient use of the fabric. The yardage given allows for the backing to be 4″ larger on all sides.

For double-fold bindings, I cut my strips 2″ wide, joining them end to end on the diagonal and pressing the binding length in half so it is 1″ wide, and then sewing it to the quilt with a ¼″ seam allowance. This gives me a nicely filled ¼″-wide finished binding that won't nip off the points of piecing that go all the way to the edge of the quilt, especially nice on a quilt with pieced borders, or without borders at all.

The yardage given within each pattern allows for cutting up to 2½″-wide binding strips if you so desire.

Specialty Rulers

FAST2CUT BONNIE K. HUNTER'S ESSENTIAL TRIANGLE TOOL

With this ruler (by C&T Publishing), I have combined the fastest way of making my favorite units accurately—with easy measuring and cutting in multiple sizes—all from one tool. My fast2cut Essential Triangle Tool is perfect for half-square triangles, quarter-square triangles, and Flying Geese units, all cut from easy strip widths.

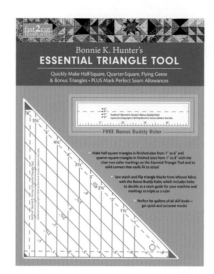

HALF-SQUARE TRIANGLES

Use the red lines and numbers.

1. Determine the finished size of the half-square triangle unit and add ½″ for the seam allowance. Cut 1 strip this width of 2 different colors. *For example:* For a half-square triangle that finishes at 2″, begin with 2½″ strips.

2. Place 2 desired fabric strips right sides together. Square off one end of the strips.

3. Find the number on the ruler that indicates the finished size of the desired unit. Place that line at the top of the strips, with the solid triangle at the tip of the ruler extending beyond the lower edge of the strips. The vertical edge of the ruler should align with the cut end of the strips. *Fig. A*

4. Cut through both layers with a rotary cutter.

5. Rotate the ruler, aligning the angled edge of the ruler with the newly cut edge of the strips. The solid triangle at the tip of the ruler will extend beyond the upper edge of the strips. *Fig. B*

6. Cut through both layers with a rotary cutter.

7. Return the ruler to position 1, repeating Steps 3–6 to cut the number of matched triangle pairs needed. Proper cutting and sewing will ensure that the units come out the correct size.

8. Cut and sew a few triangles, chain piecing them one after the other. *Fig. C*

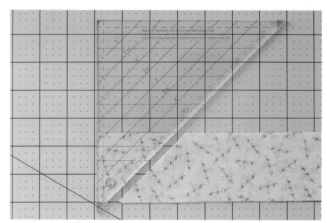

A. Half-square triangles, position 1

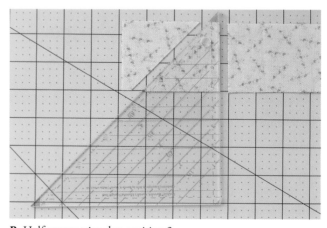

B. Half-square triangles, position 2

C

9. Press and measure. Adjust the seam allowance if needed. *Never trust a ¼″ foot.* **Fig. D**

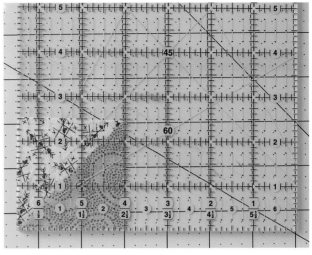

D

> ### Helpful Hints
>
> • *To convert other cutting dimensions for use with this tool, simply find the finished size of the triangle unit needed and add ½″ to this measurement to determine the strip width. If the pattern doesn't state a finished size but gives a cut measurement such as 2⅞″ or 2⅜″, simply subtract ⅜″ from the cut measurement to find the strip width you need.*
>
> • *If a pattern is having you cut oversized and "sew big to sliver trim down," find the trimmed size. This is the strip width you would cut.*

- -

QUARTER-SQUARE TRIANGLES

Use the green lines and numbers.

Quarter-square triangles are essential in quilting. They have the straight of grain on the hypotenuse, the long side, of the triangle, to prevent stretchy bias edges from being on the outside edge of your quilt or block.

Quarter-Square Triangles for Hourglass Units

Layered strips allow you to cut 2 triangles at once. When you layer 2 different fabric strips together, you'll cut pairs of triangles already matched together for sewing, making the job extra easy. The numbers along the short side of the ruler will give you the finished unit size, and the numbers in the center tell you what size strip you need to cut.

1. Cut 1 strip the width you need from each of 2 different colors. The strips shown are for a 4″ finished unit, which uses 2½″ strips.

2. Place the 2 fabric strips right sides together.

3. Position the ruler so that the desired strip-width line (in this case 2½″) is aligned with the bottom edge of the strips. The solid triangle at the tip of the ruler will extend beyond the strips. **Fig. A**

4. Cut through both layers on both sides of the ruler with a rotary cutter.

5. Rotate the ruler, aligning the angled edge of the ruler with the newly cut edge of the strips. The solid triangle at the tip of the ruler will extend beyond the bottom edge of the strips. **Fig. B**

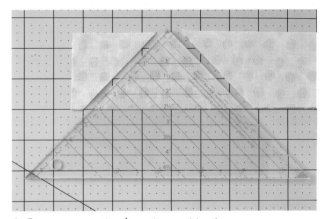

A. Quarter-square triangle cutting, position 1

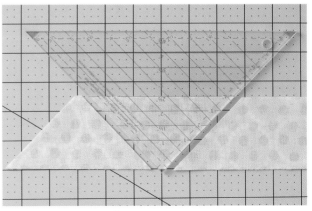

B. Quarter-square triangle cutting, position 2

6. Cut through both layers with a rotary cutter along the right side of the ruler.

7. Stitch quarter-square triangle pairs into hourglass halves, using a ¼″ seam. Press toward the darker fabric. Proper cutting and sewing will ensure that the units come out the correct size. *Fig. C*

8. Join the halves to complete each hourglass unit. Press the seams to one side. *Fig. D*

Flying Geese

Quarter-square triangles and half-square triangles are combined to make Flying Geese units quickly and easily with no waste, no drawing of lines, and best yet … from strip widths you may already have on hand!

1. Cut quarter-square triangles (center yellow triangle), following Quarter-Square Triangles for Hourglass Units, Steps 1–5 (page 9). Layer like fabric strips together if you need several of the same triangle. Layer different strips to cut 2 different triangles at once. *Fig. E*

2. Cut half-square triangles (white wing triangles) following Quarter-Square Triangles for Hourglass Units, Steps 1–7 (page 9). with one exception: Fold a single fabric strip in half, right sides together, rather than stacking 2 separate strips. This will give you 2 mirror-image triangles.

3. Position the right wing triangle and the center triangle right sides together, matching both the blunt end and the pointy tip. Starting at the blunt tip, stitch the angled side with a ¼″ seam. *Fig. F*

4. Press the seam toward the wing triangle. *Fig. G*

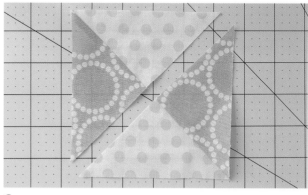

C

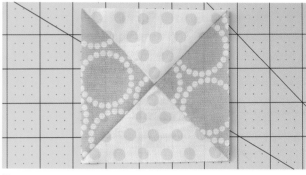

D

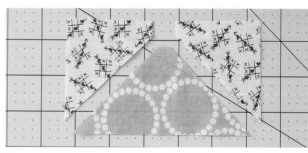

E

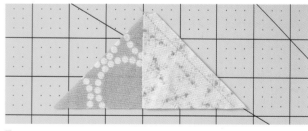

F

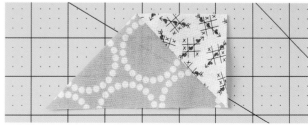

G

5. Add the left wing triangle to the center triangle, right sides together, matching points and keeping the blunt ends even. Stitch this seam from the bottom point up to the blunt top. Press the seam toward the wing triangle. Trim the dog-ears. *Figs. H & I*

Use this chart as a quick reference of strip widths for common sizes of Flying Geese units.

Finished Flying Geese unit size	Goose and wing triangle-strip width
1″ × 2″	1½″
1½″ × 3″	2″
2″ × 4″	2½″
2½″ × 5″	3″
3″ × 6″	3½″
3½″ × 7″	4″
4″ × 8″	4½″

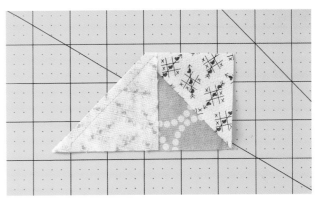

H

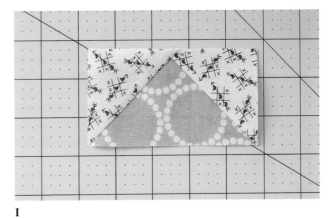

I

String Piecing Basics

Narrow strips of fabric, leftover bits from recently finished projects, pieces gifted from friends—these are the *best* parts of the scraps for me.

I'm the same way with the Thanksgiving turkey. While some like the breast meat only and throw out the rest, I find the best parts are those that remain after the big meal is over, as I think of absolutely everything I can make with every spare morsel.

Besides, the scraps cost just as much as the original yardage that they came from.

In this book, I've combined my love of strings together with recognizable traditional patchwork elements. String units mixed with other patchwork pieces add a dynamic, eye-catching feature in a scrap quilt!

WHAT IS A STRING?

Historically, the term *string* refers to a piece of fabric considered "too small" to be used in household sewing. Too insignificant for clothing construction, too tiny for household linens—these were the bits destined for the trash bin. In most cases, they were even too small to be considered as rags.

But quilters are and always have been a resilient lot and, of course, we could find a way to use them by sewing them back together into bigger pieces, trimming to shape, and adding them to each other. Patterns emerged, and with sewing the strips to a foundation of paper or fabric, these strings found places of beauty in stunning quilts from the humblest of circumstances.

Though many string quilts were simply considered to be utilitarian in nature, they hold a charm and a vibrant freedom that many other tradition-ally pieced quilts do not have.

String quilts have always been a fascination for me—the randomness of placement, the variety of color, and most of all the stories these quilts and fabrics could tell about their makers—if only quilts could talk.

How Wide Are Strings?

In my book, a string is any narrow piece of fabric ranging from ¾″ wide up to 2″ wide. Lengths can vary, but anything shorter than 5″ would be categorized by me as a "crumb" rather than a "string."

I love to vary the widths of my strips and find it fun to even lay things on a slight angle from time to time, causing the direction of the strings to tilt and lean in my block so they are not all marching in the same direction like straight little soldiers. Let them play, let them dance! The more variety in placement the better.

My string collecting is simple. I start with a basket placed under my cut-ting table and anything "string worthy" that I don't want to cut into other scrap sizes is placed into the basket. Every project leaves strings. I've such an addiction to the odd-size narrow strips that I will even move the ruler over a whole inch or so when straightening up a piece of fabric so I can save a whole string, instead of simply discarding ¼″ of trimmings. Variety is key—the more you save, the more you'll have.

When the basket is full I have a couple of choices to make—do I want to make a string quilt with all of the colors of the rainbow included? Or do I want to play with a few select color families for a more planned look?

If a quilt with a certain color scheme is at the forefront, the sorting takes place. It's a fun and messy process, the sorting of the strings. I dump the basket on the floor, and while watching a movie I sort the saved strips by color family, storing each family in its own clear plastic tub so I can see what's what and can easily dig into an evening of string piecing by color.

FOUNDATIONS

The reasons I want foundations in my string piecing are two-fold.

• A foundation stabilizes the block when working with narrow strips, especially when the strips may be slightly off grain, or not have straight edges.

• A foundation gives me a boundary to shoot for! I know the size of my block, and whether the strip will fit or not because the paper shows me the size of the unit I am making. I can very effectively use my scraps to fill the block dimensions this way.

In looking at vintage quilts, you will find any and every fabric used for foundations in string piecing, including muslin, printed cotton, batiste, lawn, and many others. In the paper foundation category, I've seen every kind of paper used—sheet music, church bulletins, newspaper, and even family letters.

I prefer to use paper foundations in my string piecing for many reasons. One reason is that I find sewing straight strips of fabric across the bias of a fabric foundation can cause warping and rolling and a foundation that won't lie flat. Paper is sturdy in every direction, having no bias.

My quilts are full of small pieces and many seams. Being able to remove the paper from the string piecing also helps eliminate excess bulk that would add more weight if I left fabric foundations in place when sewing the top together.

There are many kinds of paper suitable for string piecing. Telephone books, financial prospectus pages that come quarterly for a 401(k), doodle pads from the dollar store, and newsprint end rolls have all been used successfully in the past. Look for a thin, crisp paper that tears away easily after stitching. Tracing paper and vellum are not recommended as they may curl or shrink when touched with an iron.

There are also wonderful foundation papers available for purchase. Try Carol Doak's Foundation Paper (by C&T Publishing), especially when printing foundations where sewing on a line is necessary. It is designed for stitching and tearing away. The 8½″ × 11″ and 8½″ × 14″ sheets feed through a printer easily.

For Easy Paper Removal

Paper removal is easy if you remember the following:

• Use a size 14 needle in your machine to make bigger holes in the paper.

• Set the stitch length very small—1.5 on a digital machine or about 17 stitches per inch on a vintage machine.

Smaller stitches and bigger needle holes make the paper very easy to remove. If the paper is falling off too soon, lengthen the stitch a bit. If the stitches are too large, you may find the stitches pulling and distorting as you fight to remove the paper.

As paper is hardest to remove when seamlines cross other seamlines, I square up my blocks and remove the paper before joining units together in the quilt. Once the units are pieced, squared, and de-papered, I can simply sew them together in the quilt just like any other pieced block.

PRESSING

While piecing string blocks, I tend to work with a dry iron (no steam).

Some string blocks will have bias edges. To add stability and minimize stretch when removing paper, lightly spray the completed block with spray starch and press before trimming and paper removal.

Removing paper is an acquired technique! I find that if I place the thumbnail of my left hand on the seamline I am pulling paper away from, the stitches are held secure as I remove the paper the same way I would from a perforated notebook with my right hand. I start at one corner and work my way across the block in the reverse order that pieces were sewn.

STRING BLOCK CONSTRUCTION

1. Start by laying 2 strips right sides together, across the center of the foundation square. The pattern will tell you if you are piecing diagonally or straight across the paper. Sew the 2 pieces together through the paper, using an approximate ¼″ seam. Flip the top strip over and press. *Fig. A*

2. Continue adding strips, using a stitch-and-flip manner until the foundation is completely covered. *Fig. B*

3. Press the block well. Trim to the size desired. Carefully remove the paper. *Fig. C*

Each pattern in this book will give you the size of foundation to use as well as the trimming size to complete the blocks in each quilt.

Crumb Piecing Basics

The differences between a *string* and a *crumb* are slight, and the two terms are sometimes interchangeable. But generally, the difference is simply that a string is longer and narrower while crumbs are short and chunky.

Strings and crumbs may be used together in the same block. For instance, longer strings may be placed down the center of a diagonally pieced block, but as the strips get shorter toward the outside corners, crumbs can take their place to finish the job as only small pieces are needed.

Where do crumbs come from? Ends of strip sets, leftover triangles trimmed after joining lengths of binding or borders on the diagonal. Sometimes even leftover margins from trimming string blocks leave large enough pieces to be used again as crumbs.

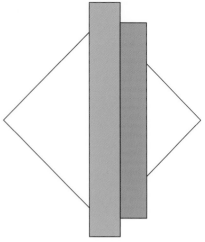

A. String block construction

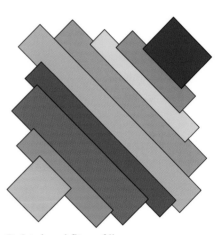

B. Stitch and flip to fill.

C. Finished string unit

FOUNDATION OR NO FOUNDATION?

The choice is up to you whether you choose to piece crumb blocks on a paper foundation or simply go paper-free. I will choose a paper foundation if my blocks need to be more than 5″ in size, simply because a foundation gives me a block that lies flatter and the paper gives me a size to shoot for, making fabric placement quick and easy.

If the block is fairly small, no foundation is necessary. I just keep a small ruler on hand to check my progress.

Remember when using a paper foundation to keep the stitch length small. Without a foundation, a short stitch is not necessary.

If you are looking to make large crumb blocks, consider sewing together several smaller ones to achieve the size block you desire. The piecing will be more interesting and it will be easier to use up smaller scraps this way rather than going too big.

BUILDING CRUMB BLOCKS

1. Start by placing 2 random scraps right sides together and stitch with an approximate ¼″ seam allowance. Pieces do not necessarily have to have straight edges, just eyeball, aim, and shoot! Trim any excess fabric away from seams pressing toward the piece just added. *Fig. D*

D. Building crumb blocks

2. Continue to add pieces to the block in a stitch-and-flip manner, trimming and pressing after the addition of each piece until you reach the desired unit size. *Fig. E*

When piecing crumb blocks, I try to avoid piecing in a circular manner leaving me with predictable blocks resembling Log Cabins. Change it up, go side by side, or opposite sides. Start in a corner, or cut across by adding a large triangle on one side. Always, always, always go for variety!

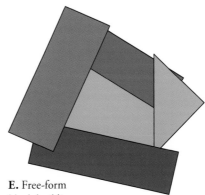

E. Free-form block building

Leftover block parts or strip sets from other projects make great additions to crumb blocks. Build around a nine-patch or a four-patch or some half-square triangles for a bit of added spark. Feel free to sew smaller scraps end to end to end to create a pieced section and then add the section onto the crumb block for a bit more unpredictability.

There really are no rules. Experiment!

3. Twist and turn the ruler on top of the block to find the most interesting placement before trimming to your desired size. *Fig. F*

F. Trim as desired.

Are the corners you trimmed off big enough to start another block center? They could be!

Geese on a String

FINISHED BLOCK: 6″ × 6″ · FINISHED QUILT: 70″ × 83″

MATERIALS

Foundation paper: 60 sheets 8½″ × 11″. Cut 42 squares 7¼″ × 7¼″ from 42 sheets of foundation paper. Cut each square on the diagonal twice to yield 168 foundation triangles. The remaining 18 sheets will be used in the string pieced border.

Assorted colorful scraps: 9½ yards for Flying Geese, four-patches, and string border

Melon solid: 2 yards for Flying Geese rows

Moss green solid: 1¼ yards for four-patch rows

Navy solid: ⅜ yard for inner border

Brown stripe: ¾ yard for binding

Backing: 5 yards

Batting: 78″ × 91″

CUTTING

Flying Geese Rows, Borders, and Binding

Cut a wide variety of neutral scraps into random widths from ¾″ to 2″ for string pieced triangles and border. Shorter strips can be joined end to end to create the needed length. Cut enough to get going; cut more variety as needed.

Melon solid

Cut 168 squares 3⅞″ × 3⅞″; subcut each square on the diagonal once to yield 336 wing triangles.

Navy solid

Cut 7 strips 1½″ × width of fabric.

Brown stripe

Cut 9 strips 2″ × width of fabric.

> ### Cutting Tip
> To cut the half-square wing triangles from 3½″ strips, I used the 3″ finished red line on my fast2cut Essential Triangle Tool (page 8).

Four-Patch Rows

The small colorful four-patches in this quilt were the perfect place to use up a bundle of saved 1½″ strips from recycled shirt fabrics left from other projects. As scraps vary in width and length, no exact number of strips to cut is given. What matters is the number of units you can get out of the strip sets you have sewn. Cut and sew, and cut some more as needed until you have reached the number of subcuts required for the 150 four-patches used in the green alternate rows in the quilt.

Colored fabric scraps

Cut several 1½″ strips.

Moss green solid

Cut 75 squares 4¼″ × 4¼″; subcut each square on the diagonal twice to yield 300 quarter-square setting triangles.

> ### Cutting Tip
> To cut the quarter-square setting triangles (page 9) from 2″ strips, I used the 3″ finished green line on my fast2cut Essential Triangle Tool (page 8).

> **NOTE:** The letters in the following instructions refer to the letters on the illustrations in this project's At a Glance (pages 20 and 21).

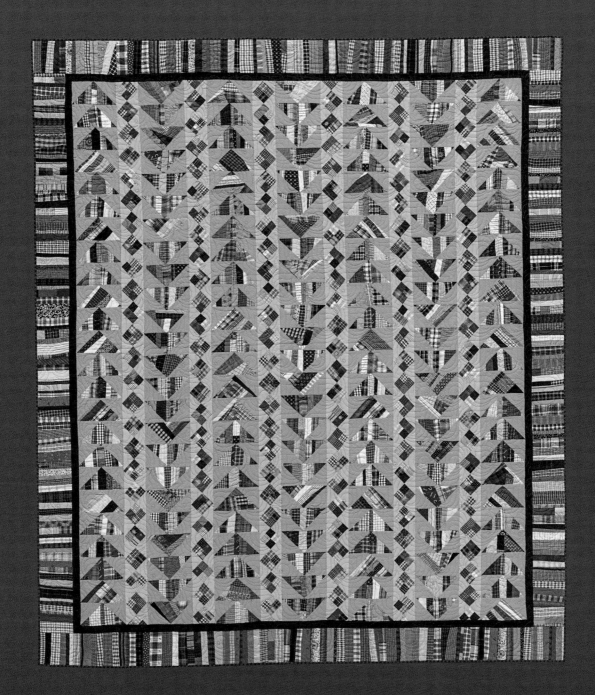

INSPIRED BY AN ANTIQUE QUILT purchased in Greensboro, North Carolina, *Geese on a String* uses leftover bits, strings, strips, and chunks from deconstructed clothing.

I love working with recycled fabrics. There is something elemental about taking a garment apart, returning it back to "fabric," and refashioning the pieces into a quilt. It's as if the fabrics tell a story as they come together.

Geese on a String uses purchased solid yardage in shades of salmon and moss green in conjunction with the recycled fabric giving it an instantly vintage yet timeless appeal!

Flying Geese Construction

The Flying Geese are created by covering a base triangle of foundation paper with the narrow strips of fabric. The paper adds stability and keeps the fabric from bunching, shifting, or warping during piecing.

A Lay the first scrap strip right side up, down the center of the paper triangle from top to bottom. Place the second strip right side down, on top of the first. The strips should slightly extend beyond the edges of the paper and will be trimmed to size later. If desired, angle the placement of the strips.

Stitch along the second strip, using a ¼″ seam. Trim the first fabric, if necessary, to leave a ¼″ seam allowance. Press to one side.

Continue to add strips to each side of the center strip until the paper triangle is completely covered. Tilting and leaning the strips with wonky angles adds more charm.

Shorter strips may be joined end to end for a length long enough to reach across the foundation from top to bottom. Let the seams fall where they may!

This is also a great place to add some crumb-pieced Flying Geese as well. Go wild with scraps and have some fun.

Make 168 base triangles.

B Trim foundations by following the edge of the paper triangles. Remove the paper.

C Add the right wing triangles to the Flying Geese base triangles with the units right sides together. Press toward the wing triangles. Repeat the process for the left wing triangles, pressing the seam toward the triangles just added. Remove the dog-ears. The units will measure 3½″ × 6½″ and finish at 3″ × 6″ in the quilt.

D Join the Flying Geese into pairs. Press the seam toward the bottom Flying Geese unit. Make 84. The blocks will measure 6½″ × 6½″ and finish at 6″ × 6″ in the quilt.

E Join 12 Flying Geese pairs into one length of 24 Flying Geese per row. Press. Make 7 rows.

Four-Patch Construction

F Match pairs of 1½″ colored strips in random fashion, sewing for as much variety as possible within the four-patch units. I find that working with short strips helps increase variety in strip sets. Press the seams to one side and measure. Strip sets should measure 2½″ wide at this point. Adjust the seam allowance if the proper width is not reached. Make several strip sets to get going, and make more as needed to achieve the number of four-patches required.

Place 2 different strip sets right sides together with the seams opposing, preparing to cut matched pairs of units ready to sew.

G Crosscut each matched strip set pair into 1½″-wide segments. Each cut will yield 1 four-patch pair ready to sew. Keep sewing and cutting strip sets as needed until you have 154 matched four-patch sets.

Sew each pair together to make a four-patch unit. Press. The units will measure 2½″ × 2½″ and finish at 2″ × 2″ in the quilt.

Following the lead of the antique quilt I purchased, I built the four-patch rows in 1 long strip and then cut the rows the length that I needed to fit between the rows of Flying Geese. This means that the rows finish or begin with partial four-patch units and every row is different, adding a bit of whimsical charm to the whole. It also solved the problem of on-point math, and I didn't have to recalculate the width of my four-patch strips so that columns would come out even. Just cut it off! It's rather freeing to the spirit!

H Add a quarter-square triangle to opposite sides of each four-patch, pressing the seams toward the triangles. The units will be parallelograms. Join the units into one length, 154 units long. Square off one end.

Measure the Flying Geese rows from top to bottom. They should be close to 72½″ in length. Cut 6 four-patch rows this length, letting the seams fall where they may.

Place the ¼″ line of a ruler against the four-patch corners and trim the excess seam allowance ¼″ beyond the corners, down the length of the rows on both sides, straightening the edges and removing the dog-ears in the process.

String Border Construction

❶ Referring to String Block Construction (page 14) for string piecing, cover 18 sheets of foundation paper 8½″ × 11″ with a variety of colored strips and with strings being placed down the 11″ length of the page. Crosscut 2 border units 5″ × 8½″ from each. Carefully remove the paper.

Join the border units end to end along 5″ sides into one length at least 290″ long. You might need to add a strip or two to make the full length. Press.

Quilt Assembly

Lay out the quilt in vertical rows, paying attention to the way the rows of Flying Geese alternate direction as shown in the quilt assembly diagram (page 21).

Join the rows, pressing the seams toward the four-patch rows, to complete the quilt center. Press.

INNER BORDER

Join the 7 navy border strips end to end, using diagonal seams, to make a strip approximately 280″ long. Press the seams open.

Lay out the quilt center on the floor, smoothing it gently. Do not tug or pull. Measure the quilt through the center from top to bottom. Cut the side inner borders this length. Sew the side borders to the quilt sides, right sides together, pinning to match the centers and ends and easing where necessary to fit. Press the seams toward the borders.

Repeat for top and bottom borders, measuring across the quilt center, including the borders just added in the measurement. Cut the top and bottom borders this length. Stitch the top and bottom inner borders to the quilt center, pinning to match centers and ends, easing where necessary to fit. Press the seams toward borders.

OUTER BORDER

Measure the quilt from top to bottom, and cut 2 side string borders this length. Sew the side borders to the quilt sides, right sides together, pinning to match centers and ends, easing where necessary to fit. Press the seams toward the inner borders.

Measure the quilt from side to side, cutting 2 top and bottom string borders this length.

Stitch the top and bottom borders to the quilt, pinning to match centers and ends, easing where necessary to fit. Press the seams toward the inner borders.

Staystitch around the edge of the quilt by machine, using a long straight stitch, to keep the seams from popping open and to minimize stretch when quilting.

Finishing

Geese on a String was machine quilted with copper-colored thread, using an edge-to-edge design called Flicker by Hermione Agee of Lorien Quilting in Australia. A brown-and-black striped binding completes the vintage appeal of this timeless string quilt.

AT A GLANCE

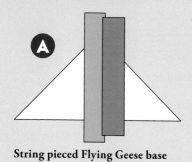

A

String pieced Flying Geese base

B

Trimmed Flying Geese triangle
Make 168.

C

Add wing triangles.
3½″ × 6½″ unfinished

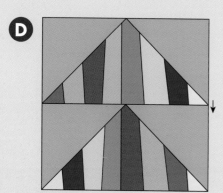

D

Joining Flying Geese
6½″ × 6½″ unfinished
Make 84.

E

Making Flying Geese rows
Make 7.

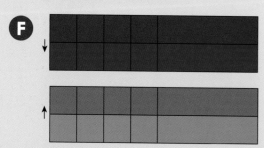

F

Four-patch strip set

G

Four-patch
Make 154.

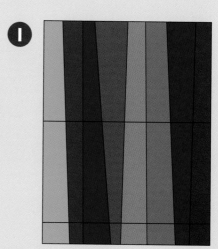

I

String border piecing

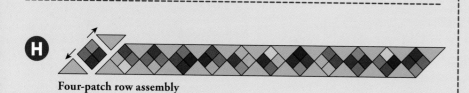
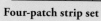

H

Four-patch row assembly

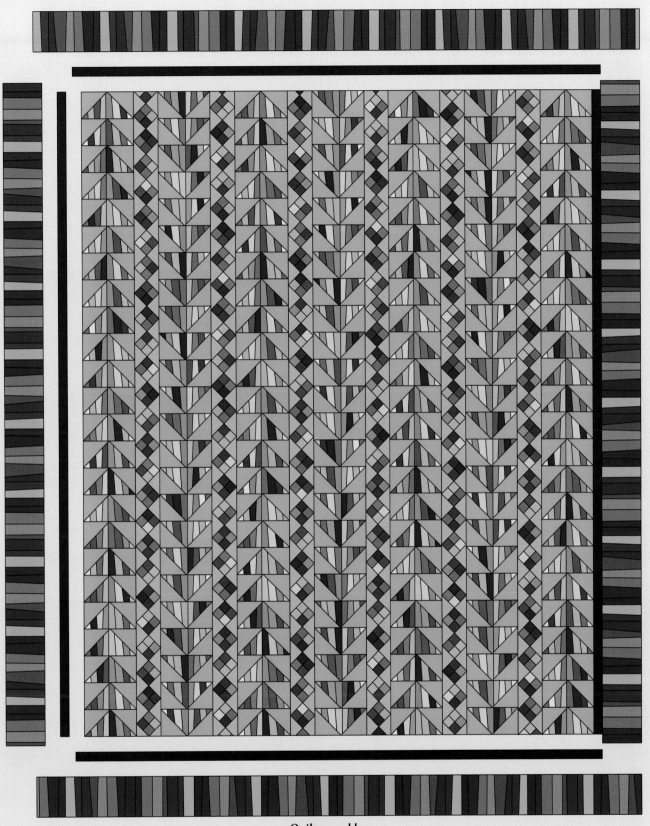

Quilt assembly

Serpentine Web

FINISHED BLOCK: 10˝ × 10˝ · FINISHED QUILT: 70˝ × 80˝

MATERIALS

Foundation paper: 115 sheets 8½˝ × 11˝. Cut 115 squares 7¾˝ × 7¾˝ from foundation paper. Cut each square on the diagonal once to yield 230 foundation triangles.

Yellow solid: 3 yards for kites

Assorted scraps from light to dark: 6½ yards for string piecing

Green print: ¾ yard for binding

Backing: 5 yards

Batting: 78˝ × 88˝

Template plastic

Glue stick

CUTTING

Yellow Solid

Trace the Serpentine Web kite pattern (page 90) onto template plastic and cut out. Fold the yellow solid fabric 4 layers thick, and trace the kite shapes onto the fabric. Use a rotary cutter and the edge of a ruler to cut the kites through all 4 layers. Cut 230 kites.

Green Print

Cut 9 strips 2˝ × width of fabric.

> **NOTE:** The letters in the following instructions refer to the letters on the illustrations in this project's At a Glance (pages 24 and 25).

Quarter-Block Construction

A Dab a few small dots of glue stick down the center of a foundation triangle from tip to base.

Place a yellow kite on top of the foundation.

Set the stitch length for stitching through paper (1.5 on a digital machine, about 17 stitches per inch). Smaller stitches make the paper easier to remove.

B Using a stitch-and-flip method, place a strip of fabric right sides together against one of the kite sides, aligning the raw edges. Stitch with a ¼˝ seam, fold the strip outward, and press. Add another strip to the opposite side of the kite to anchor the kite in place.

Continue adding strips until the whole foundation is covered. Make 218 quarter-blocks—4 for each of the 53 whole blocks and 6 used in the half-blocks.

C Trim the triangles, following the edge of the paper. Carefully remove the paper.

Go Big!

Because "shift" happens! I piece beyond my foundation triangle leaving a good ¼" of margin all around the edge of the paper. Bigger is better. Unstitching foundation piecing is no fun. I also try to have the last seam on the 2 outer corners at least 1" in from the tip to avoid bulk in this area when units come together in the block.

STRING SPIDER WEB QUILTS are traditional by description but modern in interpretation! Playing with the time-honored blocks, I found a different appearance from the norm when I set them with a half-block drop in every other row to create the serpentine effect. Give me a bucket of strings and I will happily piece myself into oblivion!

Spider Web quilts are the perfect use-it-all quilt as even small scraps can find the perfect place to

Block Assembly

D Join the quarter-blocks into 106 half-blocks, pressing the seams toward one direction. Join the half-blocks to create blocks. Due to pressing, center seams should nest.

Make 53 full blocks. Trim the blocks to 10½″ × 10½″, being sure to leave a ¼″ seam allowance beyond the points of the kites.

Half-Block Assembly

Each half-block is made with 1 quarter-block triangle and 2 mirror-image half-triangles.

E Fold the foundation and kite in half so there is a center crease from point to point.

Add strips as for quarter-block construction, only adding strips to the right of the kite on 6 foundations and adding strips to the left of the kite on the remaining 6 foundations.

Trim the strings to the edge of the paper.

Place the ¼″ line of the ruler on the fold line, down the center of the kite and trim, leaving a ¼″ seam allowance beyond the fold. Repeat for all 12 units.

Carefully remove the paper.

F Join units to complete 6 half-blocks. Trim the half-blocks to 5½″ × 10½″, being careful to leave a ¼″ seam allowance beyond the center kite point.

Quilt Assembly

Referring to the quilt assembly diagram (next page), lay out the blocks in columns with 8 blocks in each odd-numbered column, starting and ending each of 3 even-numbered columns with a half-block.

Join the blocks into columns. Press. Join the columns into the quilt center. Press.

Staystitch around the edge of the quilt to minimize stretch when quilting.

Finishing

Serpentine Web was machine quilted in yellow thread, using an edge-to-edge design called Woven Wind by Apricot Moon Designs. The colorful quilt is bound in green print to bring out the other greens within the string piecing.

AT A GLANCE

A

Fabric kite placement

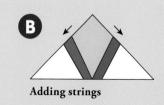

B

Adding strings

C

Filling and trimming triangle
Make 218.

D

Full Spider Web block
10½″ × 10½″ unfinished
Make 53.

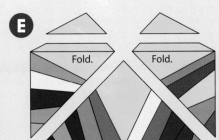

E

Fold.　　Fold.

Units for Spider Web half-block

F

Spider Web half-block
5½″ × 10½″ unfinished
Make 6.

Quilt assembly

Straits of Mackinac

FINISHED BLOCK: 12˝ × 12˝ · FINISHED QUILT: 94˝ × 94˝

MATERIALS

Foundation paper: 117 sheets 8½˝ × 11˝

Assorted aqua to turquoise scraps: 7¾ yards

Assorted neutral scraps: 10½ yards

Aqua stripe: ¾ yard for binding

Backing: 7½ yards

Batting: 102˝ × 102˝

CUTTING

Cutting Tip

To cut the many needed half-square triangles in this quilt, I used 2½˝ strips and the 2˝ finished red line on my fast2cut Essential Triangle Tool (page 8). It is so much easier to cut from than to cut from 2⅞˝ × 2⅞˝ squares. And if you layer 2 strips right sides together, pairs of triangles are cut already together and ready to sew.

Aqua to Turquoise Scraps

Cut 360 squares 2⅞˝ × 2⅞˝; subcut each square on the diagonal once to yield 720 half-square triangles.

Cut 49 squares 2½˝ × 2½˝ for cornerstones.

Neutral Scraps

Cut 288 squares 2⅞˝ × 2⅞˝; subcut each square on the diagonal once to yield 576 half-square triangles.

Cut 36 squares 3⅜˝ × 3⅜˝ for block centers.

Cut 144 rectangles 3˝ × 6˝; place 2 rectangles right sides together and cut on the diagonal once to yield 266 mirror image pairs of triangles for star point foundation piecing.

Cut 532 rectangles 2˝ × 4˝; place 2 rectangles right sides together and cut on the diagonal once to yield 288 mirror image pairs of triangles for sashing unit foundation piecing.

Aqua Stripe

Cut 11 strips 2˝ × width of fabric.

Cutting Hint

Cut aqua/turquoise and neutral strips into random widths from ¾˝ to 2˝ for string-pieced units. Strips needed will get shorter as you cover the base triangles, so any length of strip can be used. Cut enough to get going; cut more variety as needed.

THE STRAITS OF MACKINAC are a series of narrow waterways in Michigan. Every year, the Grand Hotel hosts a needle art seminar, and I've been lucky enough to teach there on multiple occasions. The main star block in this quilt was featured under the same name in *Quiltmaker* Magazine's *100 Blocks by 100 Designers, Volume 14*, after my last visit to Mackinac Island. After making just one block I knew that I had to keep sewing until I had enough for a full quilt.

Paper-piecing patterns are provided for the 4″ finished star point units and 2″ finished sashing units in this quilt. For quilters familiar with the Tri-Recs Tools (by EZ Quilting), you may also use these for trimming the string pieced center triangles and star points to the shapes required in lieu of paper piecing.

Preparing Foundations

Trace or copy 144 of the Straits of Mackinac Star Point Foundation pattern (page 91) and 532 of the Sashing and Border Unit foundation pattern (page 92), using printer paper, tracing paper, tissue, or the foundation paper of your choice. Due to the many seams in this quilt and the number of seam allowances adding bulk, I do not recommend piecing on a fabric or other leave-in foundation, making things even more bulky. I prefer to use paper and remove it before the block and quilt assembly.

Paper-Piecing Basics

There are many how-to books on paper piecing available, including best-selling titles from Carol Doak by C&T Publishing. Here are a few hints and helps from my own experience.

Piece It Random!

The stitching lines on the shaded areas on the 4″ finished star point foundation are for guidance only. I randomly filled the area with different sizes of strips, so the seams fell in different places and the piecing on each triangle unit is different. I did stitch the smaller 2″ finished sashing units with 2 pieces of aqua in each center section.

These units can also be cut using Tri-Recs Tools (by EZ Quilting). Keep in mind that the units are 4½″ unfinished and 2½″ unfinished.

1. Begin by centering the first piece of fabric behind area #1 on the foundation, placing the wrong side of the fabric against the unprinted side of the foundation. Look through the foundation, holding it up to the light or toward a window, and position it so there is at least ¼″ seam allowance extending beyond the line, separating area #1 from area #2. A small dot of glue stick can hold the fabric in place—pins can distort paper.

2. Place the next piece of fabric (for area #2) against the area #1 fabric, right sides together, extending the seam allowance beyond the piecing line. Cutting pieces larger than needed will make positioning easier.

3. As you add fabrics to the block for each step, place them in the correct position on the unprinted side of the foundation. Holding the block up toward a window or other light source can help with piece placement. Fill the center area of the large triangle with random widths of strips as desired.

4. Sew the star point seams by stitching directly on the line on the printed side of the foundation, extending the seamline a few stitches into the seam allowance at either end of the seam. Future seamlines will cross these and lock them in place. Backstitching is not necessary.

5. Press each seam after it has been sewn. Use a dry, warm iron, making sure that each seam is pressed completely to the side. Any tucks or pleats created during pressing could be locked in place by the next seam that crosses over and will affect the accuracy of the points or corners within the block.

6. Fold the paper back along the seam just sewn, and trim each seam as each piece is added. Because these blocks are so small, and string quilts can be heavy, I trimmed a bit smaller than the traditional ¼″ seam, but kept the seam allowance more than ⅛″. I tend to trim with scissors right over my trash can, rather than taking the time to lay everything back on a mat with a ruler and rotary cutter. You will get good at eyeballing where to trim.

If while sewing, you find yourself with a torn foundation, grab some printer mailing labels, cut them into narrow strips and use those like "adhesive bandages" to hold the foundations back together. These won't melt when being touched with the iron, as regular tape will.

7. After piecing, trim each unit by placing the ¼″ line of a ruler on the outermost seamline of the block, trimming each unit ¼″ beyond the seamline. At this point, before assembling the quilt, carefully remove all of the paper.

8. It is very easy to chain piece the neutral star point triangles in place after all of the center sections are sewn.

> **NOTE:** The letters in the following instructions refer to the letters on the illustrations in this project's At a Glance (pages 31–33).

Star Block Construction

STAR POINT UNIT

A Referring to Paper-Piecing Basics (previous page), cover the center triangle section of the foundation in a stitch-and-flip manner, trimming the seam allowances and pressing as you sew, extending the ends of each strip an approximate ¼" into the star point area of the foundation.

Add the neutral star point triangles to the unit, trimming the seam allowances and pressing after each piece is added.

Trim each unit by placing the ¼" line of a ruler on the outermost seamline of the block and cutting ¼" beyond the seamline. The units will measure 4½" × 4½" and finish at 4" × 4" in the quilt. Make 144.

CORNER TRIANGLE UNIT

B Stitch together a neutral half-square triangle and an aqua half-square triangle. Press the seam toward the aqua. Remove the dog-ears. Make 576. The units will measure 2½" × 2½" and finish at 2" × 2" in the quilt.

C Join 4 random half-square triangle units. Press. The units should measure 4½" × 4½" and finish at 4" × 4" in the quilt. Make 144.

BLOCK CENTER UNIT

D Stitch aqua half-square triangles to 2 opposite sides of a 3⅜" × 3⅜" center square. Press the seams toward the square. Add triangles to the remaining sides of the square. Press the seams toward the triangles. Remove the dog-ears. The units will measure 4½" × 4½" and finish at 4" × 4" in the quilt. Make 36.

BLOCK ASSEMBLY

E Arrange the 9 units and join them into 3 rows, pressing the seams toward star point units. Sew the rows together. Press the last 2 seams toward the center. The blocks will measure 12½" × 12½" and finish at 12" × 12" in the quilt. Make 36.

Sashings

SASHING UNIT

> *Piecing Hint*
>
> *This unit may be paper pieced, or you may use Tri-Recs Tools (by EZ Quilting) for rotary cutting. The center triangle for the sashing unit may be cut from strip sets made from pairs of 1½" aqua strips stitched together. Strip sets will measure 2½" tall. Neutral side triangles may also be cut from 2½" strips using the tools.*

F If paper piecing, refer to Paper-Piecing Basics (previous page). Cover the center triangle section of the foundation with aqua scraps in a stitch-and-flip manner, trimming the seam allowances and pressing as you sew, extending the ends of each strip an approximate ¼" into the star point area of the foundation.

Add 1 mirror-image pair of star point triangles to the unit, trimming the seam allowances as each piece is added and pressing after each seam.

Trim each unit by placing the ¼" line of a ruler on the outermost seamline of the block, trimming each unit ¼" beyond the seamline. The units will measure 2½" × 2½" and finish at 2" × 2" in the quilt—504 units will be used in the sashings and 28 units used in the border. Make 532.

SASHING ASSEMBLY

G Join 6 sashing units to complete each sashing. Press. Make 84.

Border

STRING PIECED BORDER SECTIONS

H Cover 19 sheets of 8½" × 11" foundation paper with neutral strings. Cut 2 border units 4½" × 8½" from each. Carefully remove the paper.

Join the border units end to end into one length, approximately 304" long. Press.

Cut 24 border sections 4½" × 12½" from the border length. Extra length has been added to help avoid seams too close to the ends of border sections.

BORDER SPACER UNITS

I With or without paper foundations, join 3 small neutral scraps together in random fashion, making a piece large enough to trim to 2½″ × 2½″. Press. Trim. Make 28.

J Join a sashing/border unit to a border spacer unit. Press. Make 28.

BORDER CORNER UNITS

K Cut 4 foundation paper 5″ × 5″ squares and cover with strings. Trim units to 5″ × 5″. Carefully remove the paper.

L Place 2 corner squares right sides together, with both squares having strips upright. Cut both blocks on the diagonal to yield 2 matched pairs of border corners ready to sew. Repeat with the remaining 2 corner squares.

M Stitch together a triangle pair with a ¼″ seam. Press to one side. Repeat with the remaining triangle pairs to make 4 corner units. Trim units to 4½″ × 4½″.

Cutting Tip

To easily cut the half-square triangle pairs, I placed the extra 4½″ widths of string-pieced border with right sides together, and I used the 4″ finished red line on my fast2cut Essential Triangle Tool (page 8).

BORDER ASSEMBLY

N Alternate 7 border spacer units with 6 border sections to create 1 length. Press.

Make 4.

O Add a border corner to either end of 2 of the border lengths, for top and bottom borders. Press.

Quilt Assembly

Arrange the blocks, sashings, and cornerstones as shown in the quilt assembly diagram (page 33).

Join the units into rows, pressing the seams toward the blocks and cornerstones. Join the rows to complete the quilt center. Press.

Add the side borders to the quilt, pinning to match centers and ends, easing where necessary to fit. Press the seams toward the borders.

Join the top and bottom borders to the quilt in the same manner. Press.

Finishing

Straights of Mackinac was machine quilted with aqua thread, using an edge-to-edge design called Aurora by Patricia E. Ritter and Valerie Smith. I love the watery wavy effect this design gives to the quilt. An aqua striped binding is the perfect finish!

AT A GLANCE

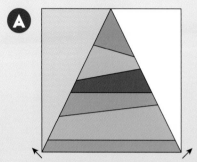

A

Star point unit
4½″ × 4½″ unfinished
Make 144.

B

Half-square triangle unit
2½″ × 2½″ unfinished
Make 576.

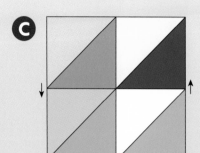

C

Block corner unit
4½″ × 4½″ unfinished
Make 144.

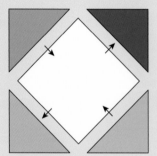

D

Block center unit
4½″ × 4½″ unfinished
Make 36.

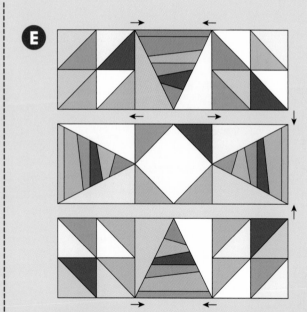

E

Block assembly
12½″ × 12½″ unfinished
Make 36.

F

Sashing unit
2½″ × 2½″ unfinished
Make 532.

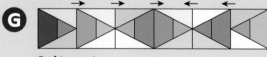

G

Sashing unit
Make 84.

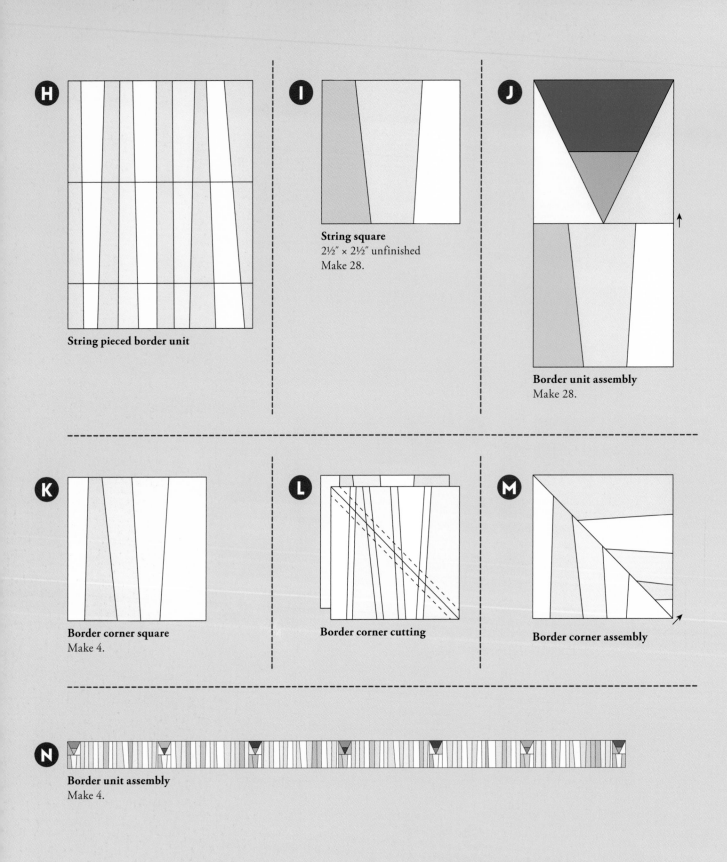

H

String pieced border unit

I

String square
2½″ × 2½″ unfinished
Make 28.

J

Border unit assembly
Make 28.

K

Border corner square
Make 4.

L

Border corner cutting

M

Border corner assembly

N

Border unit assembly
Make 4.

O

Border unit assembly

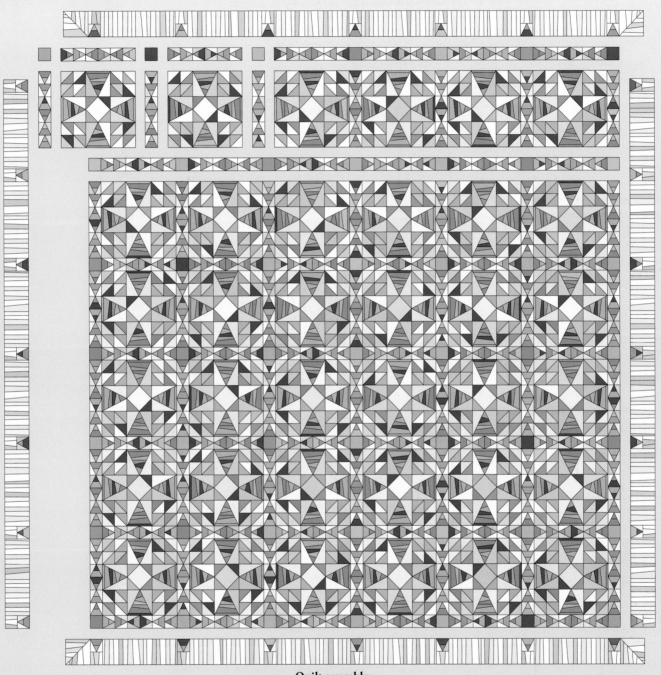

Quilt assembly

Sand Castles

FINISHED BLOCK: 10˝ × 10˝ • FINISHED QUILT: 80˝ × 80˝

MATERIALS

Foundation paper: 64 squares 6½˝ × 6½˝ (Try Carol Doak's legal sized Foundation Paper by C&T Publishing. Each 8½˝ × 14˝ sheet will yield 2 squares.)

Assorted neutral scraps: 2¾ yards for blocks

Assorted colored scraps: 4¾ yards for blocks

Taupe to sand to tan colored scraps: 4½ yards for string triangles

Wild raspberry print: ¾ yard for binding

Backing: 7½ yards

Batting: 88˝ × 88˝

CUTTING

Block Four-Patches

Four-patches are my absolute favorite patchwork unit. They liven up even the humblest of quilts! As scraps vary in width and length, no exact number of strips to cut is given. What matters is the number of units you can get out of the strip sets you have sewn. Cut, sew, and cut some more as needed until you have reached the number of subcuts required for the 512 four-patches in the blocks.

Neutral fabric:

Cut several 1½˝ strips.

Colored fabric:

Cut several 1½˝ strips.

Block Backgrounds

Colored fabric:

Cut 64 sets of 5 squares 2½˝ × 2½˝ and 3 squares 2⅞˝ × 2⅞˝; subcut each square on the diagonal once to yield 6 half-square corner triangles per block.

> ### Cutting Tip
>
> *To cut the half-square corner triangles from the same 2½˝ strip used to cut the block background squares, I used the 2˝ finished red line on my fast2cut Essential Triangle Tool (page 8).*

Block Sashings

Neutral fabric:

Cut 64 matching pairs of 2 strips 1˝ × 9½˝.

String Triangles

Taupe / sand / tan scraps:

Cut into random widths from ¾˝ to 2˝ for string triangles. Short strips can be joined end to end to create the needed length to reach across the paper and add more interest. Cut enough to get going; cut more variety as needed.

Binding

Wild raspberry print:

Cut 9 strips 2˝ × width of fabric.

> **NOTE:** The letters in the following instructions refer to the letters on the illustrations in this project's At a Glance (pages 38 and 39).

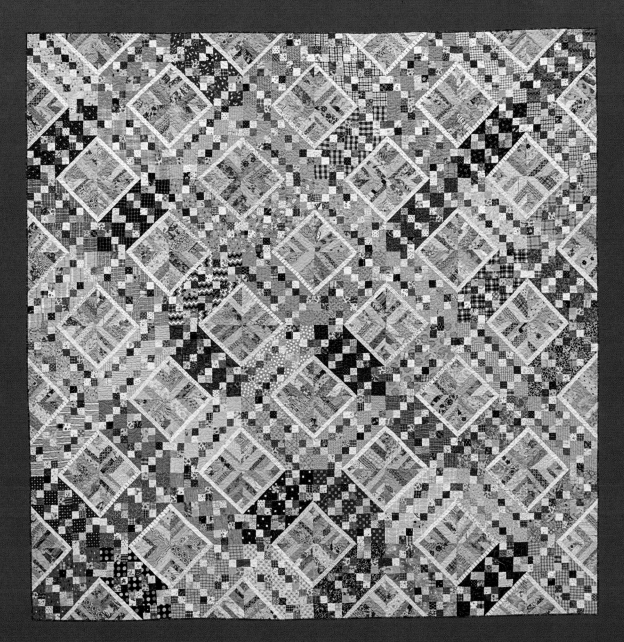

HAVING GROWN UP IN BEAUTIFUL SAN JOSE, CALIFORNIA, I have vivid memories of weekends at the beach in Santa Cruz, building sand castles with my two younger brothers. A yellow pail. A red shovel. And plenty of imagination! Oh, we had so much fun getting so gritty dirty! And we made so many great memories in the process.

My string bins are constantly burgeoning, which is a great thing—I love the inspiration that these pieces provide. When my neutral bin would not allow me to close the lid, I separated further, moving the toasty taupes and tans to their own container. There were so *many*! And that is when I decided these warmer scraps would play background to a block idea I already had on the fire.

Sand Castles recalls those long summer days and cool summer nights, complete with marshmallow roasting and s'mores aplenty.

I dedicate this quilt to the wonderful memories made with my younger brother Mark Wilkinson who left us far too soon. Mark, you are always in my heart.

Block Construction

FOUR-PATCH UNITS

(A) Match 1½″ neutral strips with 1½″ colored strips in random fashion, and sew together in pairs for as much variety as possible within the four-patch units. I find that working with short strips helps increase variety in strip sets. Press the seams toward the darker strips and measure. Strip sets should measure 2½″ wide at this point. Adjust the seam allowance if the proper width is not reached. Make several strip sets to get going, and make more as needed to achieve the number of four-patches required.

Place 2 different strip sets right sides together, with the seams opposing, preparing to cut matched pairs of units ready to sew.

Crosscut each matched strip set into 1½″-wide segments. Each cut will yield a four-patch pair ready to sew. Keep sewing and cutting strip sets, as needed, until you have 512 matched four-patch sets.

(B) Sew each pair together to make a four-patch unit. Press the seams in a circular fashion for easier nesting of patches in the quilt assembly. The units will measure 2½″ × 2½″ and finish at 2″ × 2″ in the block. Make 512.

BLOCK CENTERS

Each block will use 8 four-patch units and 1 block background set.

(C) Lay out the units into rows. Join the units into rows, pressing the seams toward the background patches. Join the rows to complete the block center. Press. Make 64.

STRING TRIANGLES

(D) Referring to String Piecing Basics (page 11), cover the 64 paper foundations 6½″ × 6½″ in a stitch-and-flip manner, pressing and trimming after each seam until the paper foundations are covered.

Trim the blocks to 6½″ × 6½″. Cut each block on the diagonal once to yield 128 string triangles. Carefully remove the paper.

BLOCK ASSEMBLY

The sashing strips are longer than the triangles and will be trimmed after piecing.

(E) Join a matching set of 1″ × 9½″ strips to the long side of 2 random string triangles. Press the seams toward the sashings.

(F) Trim the ends of the strips even with the right angles of the triangle. The triangles will be oversized and trimmed after adding to the block centers.

(G) Match the centers of the triangle sashing to the block centers. Stitch. Press the seams toward the string triangles.

(H) Trim the block to 10½″ × 10½″. The blocks will finish at 10″ × 10″ in the quilt. Make 64.

Quilt Assembly

Lay out the blocks, rotating them to complete the design as shown in the quilt assembly diagram (page 39).

Join the blocks into rows, pressing the seams in an opposing manner so the rows will nest.

Join the rows to complete the quilt top. Press.

Staystitch around the edge of the quilt by machine, using a long straight stitch, to keep the seams from popping open and to minimize stretch when quilting.

Finishing

Sand Castles was machine quilted with sand colored thread using an edge-to-edge design called Dusty Miller Grande by Patricia E. Ritter of Urban Elementz. A wild raspberry print binding brings a pop color to the edge of the quilt.

AT A GLANCE

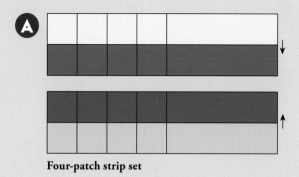

A

Four-patch strip set

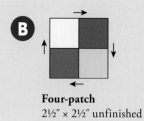

B

Four-patch
2½″ × 2½″ unfinished
Make 512.

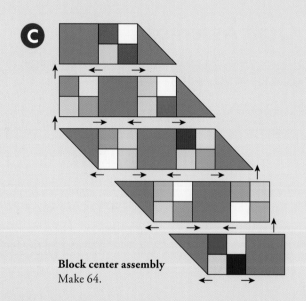

C

Block center assembly
Make 64.

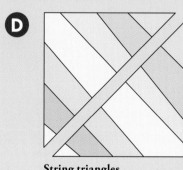

D

String triangles
Make 128.

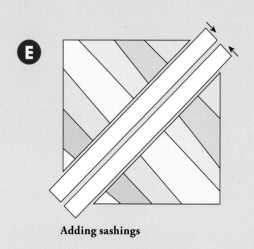

E

Adding sashings

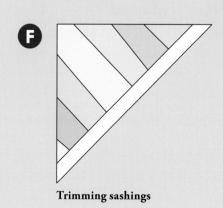

F

Trimming sashings

G

Adding triangles to block

H

Trimming block
10½″ × 10½″ unfinished
Make 64.

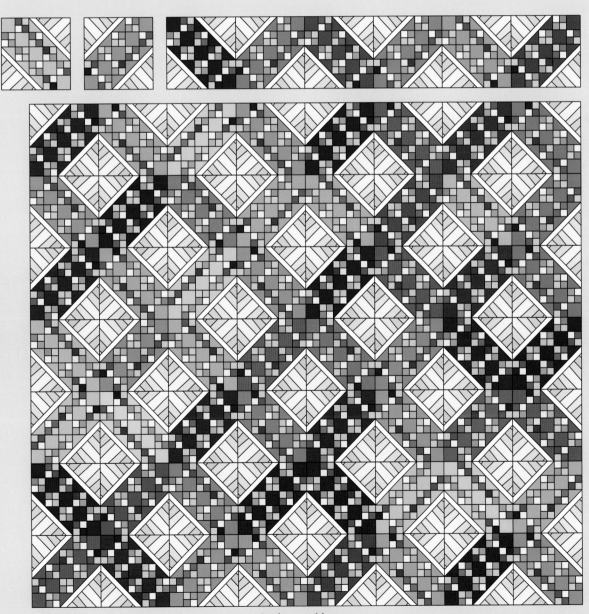

Quilt assembly

Silver Linings

FINISHED BLOCK: 12″ × 12″ • FINISHED QUILT: 84″ × 84″

MATERIALS

I dug into my 2″ strips bins for the making of the red-and-neutral blocks in this quilt. Variety is the key to everything, and having these readily available in my Scrap User's System meant I was off and sewing in no time at all.

Foundation paper: 98 squares 7″ × 7″ (Try Carol Doak's Legal-Size Foundation Paper, by C&T Publishing. You can get 2 squares out of an 8½″ × 14″ sheet.)

Assorted red scraps: 4 yards for blocks and binding

Assorted light neutral scraps: 2¾ yards for blocks

Assorted gray scraps and strings: 7 yards for setting triangles

Backing: 7¾ yards

Batting: 92″ × 92″

CUTTING

As the reds and neutrals in the album blocks are extremely scrappy, I found it helpful to cut for each block individually, pinning parts for each block together before sewing.

Full Blocks

Cutting is for 1 full block.
Cut a total of 46 sets of patches.

Red scraps:

Cut 21 squares 2″ × 2″.

Light neutral scraps:

Cut 8 squares 2″ × 2″.

Cut 4 strips 2″ × 5″.

Half-Blocks

Cutting is for 1 half-block.
Cut a total of 6 sets of patches.

Red scraps:

Cut 13 squares 2″ × 2″.

Light neutral scraps:

Cut 5 squares 2″ × 2″.

Cut 2 rectangles 2″ × 3½″.

Cut 1 strip 2″ × 5″.

Block Corner Triangles

Gray scraps:

Cut strips into random widths from ¾″ to 2″ for string pieced setting triangles. As strips needed will get shorter as you cover the base squares, any length of strip can be used. Shorter strips can also be joined end to end to create the needed length. Cut enough to get going; cut more variety as needed.

Binding

Assorted red scraps:

Cut 9 strips 2″ × width of fabric.

> **NOTE:** The letters in the following instructions refer to the letters on the illustrations in this project's At a Glance (pages 44 and 45).

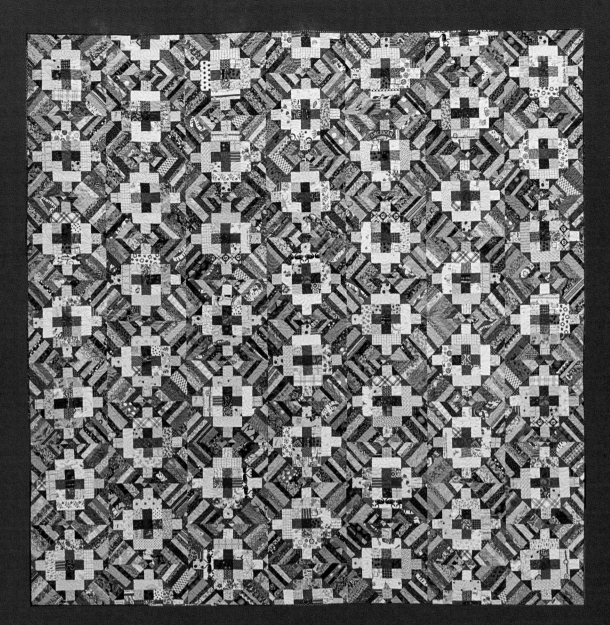

THIS QUILT COULD ALSO BE TITLED *I Get by with a Little Help from My Friends*!

At the tail end of our Allietare Mystery Quilt in January 2016, which used gray yardage as part of the quilt, I had put out on my blog that I was looking for "gray strings" for a project. My intention was that those who were cleaning up from their own Allietare quilts would slip a couple of leftover gray strips or strings into a standard sized envelope and mail them to me with a regular stamp.

I was not prepared for the windfall of blessings that came my way from across the country and around the globe. In fact, it wasn't just strings or strips that found their way to me in North Carolina—it was fat quarters, half-yards, recycled clothing pieces, strips, strings, squares, rectangles, and everything in between. This global love filled two laundry baskets and I am still sewing from it today. Some of these gray pieces are also found in *Punkin' Patch* (page 78).

I dedicate *Silver Linings* to those who lifted me through the gift of fabric when my heart needed it the most.

Full Block Construction

A Lay out 5 red and 4 neutral 2″ × 2″ squares. Join the squares into rows and press the seams. Join the rows to complete a unit. Press the seams toward the center row. Make 46.

B Join 2 red 2″ × 2″ squares to a center neutral 2″ × 2″ square. Press the seams toward the red. Center a red square over the top of the neutral square and stitch. The edge of the unit will have a stair-step appearance. Press. Make 4 corner units per block.

Add a neutral 2″ × 5″ strip to the bottom of 2 of the units. Press the seam toward the neutral strip.

Stitch red squares to both ends of 2 neutral 2″ × 5″ strips. Press the seams toward the red squares. Join these 2 units to the bottom of the 2 remaining corner units. Press the seams toward the neutral strip. Make 4 per block.

C Add the 2 smaller corner units to either side of the nine-patch center, pressing the seams toward the neutral strips. Add the larger units in the same manner, also pressing toward the neutral strips. Repeat for all 46 full blocks.

D Place the ¼″ line of a ruler along the corners of the neutral points at the edge of the block and trim, leaving a ¼″ seam allowance beyond all corners. The blocks should measure approximately 9″ × 9″ and finish at 8½″ × 8½″ in the quilt. Trim 46 blocks.

Half-Block Construction

The half-blocks are assembled much like the full blocks, starting with a partial nine-patch.

E Join 3 red 2″ × 2″ squares side by side. Press the seams toward the outer squares. Join 2 neutral 2″ × 2″ squares to a center red 2″ × 2″ square. Press the seams toward the center square. Join the rows to create a partial nine-patch. Make 6.

Sew together 2 red squares, 1 white square, and 1 white 2″ × 3½″ rectangle to make a side unit. Make 6 each of the left and right side units.

Sew together 5 red squares, 1 white square, and 1 white 2″ × 5″ rectangle to make a top unit. Make 6.

Sew the side units to a partial nine-patch. Add the top unit. Make 6 half-blocks.

F Referring to Full Block Construction (at left), trim the 2 stair-step sides of the half-blocks. The blocks are slightly oversized in height and will be trimmed when the quilt top is complete.

String Block Corner Triangles

G Referring to String Piecing Basics (page 11), cover the 98 paper foundations in a stitch-and-flip manner, pressing and trimming after each seam until the paper foundations are covered.

Trim the blocks to 7″ × 7″.

H Cut each block on the diagonal once to yield 196 string triangles. Carefully remove the paper. The triangles will be a bit oversize and trimmed after the block columns are pieced.

Block Row Construction

I Join 4 corner triangles and 1 block. Press the seams toward the corner triangles. Trim each block to 12½″ × 12½″ keeping a ¼″ seam allowance beyond the red triangle on each side. Make 46.

J Join 2 corner triangles to a half-block. Press toward the corner triangle. The block will be trimmed to size after quilt assembly. Make 6, a pair in each even-numbered row.

K Join 7 full blocks. Press the seams toward the corner triangles. Make 4 odd-numbered rows.

L Join 2 half-block row end units and 6 full blocks. Press. Make 3 even-numbered rows.

Quilt Assembly

Lay out the odd- and even-numbered rows as shown in the quilt assembly diagram (page 45), matching the red triangle in the half-block rows to the seams in the full block rows. The half-block rows will be slightly longer, and trimmed after assembly.

Join the rows to complete the quilt top. Use a long ruler to trim half-block rows even with the full block rows.

Staystitch around the edge of the quilt by machine, using a long straight stitch, to keep the seams from popping open and to minimize stretch when quilting.

Finishing

Silver Linings was machine quilted in gray thread, using an edge-to-edge design called Marmalade by Patricia E. Ritter and Leisha Farnsworth of Urban Elementz. I joined assorted red 2″ strips on the diagonal to create a scrappy binding with a ¼″ finish that also helped clean off my cutting table in the process.

On the Flip Side!

Leftover string blocks and 2″ strips of red and neutral fabrics extended the fabric needed for the back, making it just big enough and adding a bit more interest! Why put it back in the stash? Use it up on the back!

Quilt back piecing

AT A GLANCE

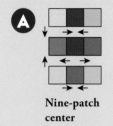

A

Nine-patch center

B

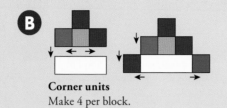

Corner units
Make 4 per block.

C

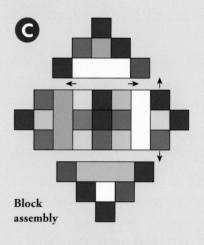

Block assembly

D

Full block trimming

E

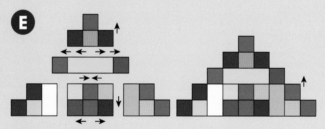

Half-block assembly

F

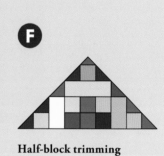

Half-block trimming

G

String block
7″ × 7″ unfinished
Make 98.

H

Corner triangles
Make 196.

I

Full block unit
Make 46.

J

Half-block unit
Make 6.

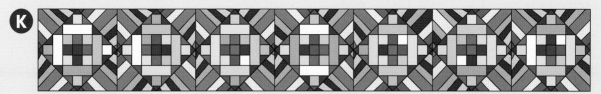

Full block row

Half-block row

Quilt assembly

Dawn's Early Light

FINISHED BLOCK: 24˝ × 24˝ • FINISHED QUILT: 88˝ × 88˝

MATERIALS

Foundation paper: 78 sheets
8½˝ × 11˝. Cut 36 squares 7˝ × 7˝,
84 squares 4½˝ × 4½˝, and
144 squares 3½˝ × 3½˝.

**Assorted neutral scraps
and strings:** 8¾ yards

Assorted red fabrics:
3 yards

**Assorted blue fabrics
and strings:** 4 yards

Blue print: ¾ yard
for binding

Backing: 8 yards

Batting: 96˝ × 96˝

CUTTING

> ### Cutting Tip
>
> *To cut the many needed half-square triangles in this quilt, I used 1½˝ and 2½˝ strips and then used the 1˝ and 2˝ finished red lines respectively on my fast2cut Essential Triangle Tool (page 8). It is so much easier to cut from strips than to cut from squares. And pairs of triangles are cut with right sides already together and ready to sew.*

Assorted neutral fabrics:

Cut 320 squares 1⅞˝ × 1⅞˝; subcut
each square on the diagonal once
to yield 640 half-square triangles.

Cut 184 squares 1½˝ × 1½˝.

Cut 264 rectangles 1½˝ × 2½˝.

Cut 60 strips 1½˝ × 4½˝.

Cut 108 squares 2⅞˝ × 2⅞˝; subcut
each square on the diagonal once
to yield 216 half-square triangles.

Cut 9 strips 1½˝ × width of fabric.

Assorted red fabrics:

Cut 320 squares 1⅞˝ × 1⅞˝; subcut
each square on the diagonal once
to yield 640 half-square triangles.

Cut 604 squares 1½˝ × 1½˝.

Cut 84 strips 1½˝ × 6½˝.

Assorted blue fabrics:

Cut 216 squares 2⅞˝ × 2⅞˝;
subcut each square on the
diagonal once to yield
432 half-square triangles.

String preparation:

Cut neutral and blue scraps into
random widths from ¾˝ to 2˝
for string piecing the block and
border units. Short strips can be
used by joining them end to end
to create the needed length to
reach across the paper foundation and add more interest to the
blocks. Cut enough to get going;
cut more variety as needed.

Blue print:

Cut 10 strips 2˝ × width of
fabric.

NOTE: The letters in the following instructions refer to the letters on
the illustrations in this project's At a Glance (pages 50 and 51).

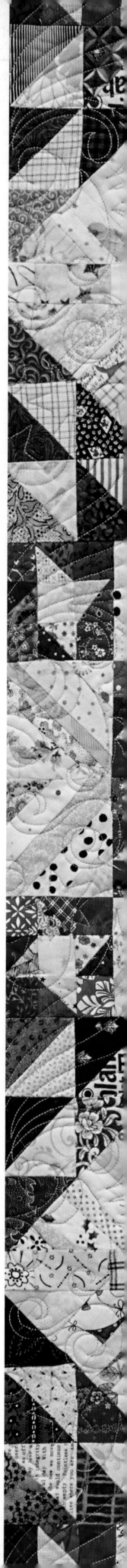

THERE IS NOTHING SO SIMPLY CLASSIC AS A RED, WHITE, AND BLUE QUILT.

It brings to mind visions of 4th of July parades, the most memorable of my youth happening in 1976 as America's bicentennial birthday build-up had been ramping up all through the year. You should have seen the red and white striped bell bottoms I was so proud to wear—complete with white stars on a field of blue fabric as pockets.

I love red, white, and blue. And I had so much fun making this quilt! This is a great one to really push your boundaries when it comes to those neutral string blocks. Whites, creams, and beiges—and many of them have other colors besides red or blue playing on them. Be sure to check out the close-up photos—and dig into your neutral stash with abandon!

Block Construction

NEUTRAL STRING SQUARES

Ⓐ Referring to String Piecing Basics (page 11), cover the 3½″ × 3½″ paper foundations in a stitch-and-flip manner, pressing and trimming after each seam until the foundation squares are covered. Trim the blocks to 3½″ × 3½″. Carefully remove the paper. Make 144.

NEUTRAL STRING TRIANGLES

Ⓑ As in Step A, cover a 7″ × 7″ foundation square with fabric strips and strings. Make 36. Trim to 6⅞″ × 6⅞″. Cut on the diagonal across the strings to yield 72 string triangles. Carefully remove the paper.

STARS AND STRINGS UNITS

Trimming Needed?

It isn't necessary to go big to sliver-trim down. Just scant the seam allowance a bit, and there will be plenty of margin to trim if you are a compulsive trimmer.

Ⓒ Match a neutral and a red 1⅞″ half-square triangle and stitch them together. Press the seam toward the red. Remove the dog-ears and trim to 1½″ × 1½″ if needed. Make 640. Each of the 9 blocks will need 64 of these half-square triangle units, with the rest being used in the sashings and border. The units will measure 1½″ × 1½″ and finish at 1″ × 1″ in the quilt.

Ⓓ Arrange 4 half-square triangle units, 4 red 1½″ × 1½″ squares, and 1 neutral 1½″ × 1½″ center square, paying attention to the way the triangles turn. Join the units into rows, pressing the seams toward the squares to facilitate nested seams. Join the rows to complete the star. Make 144. The units will measure 3½″ × 3½″ and finish at 3″ × 3″ in the quilt.

Ⓔ Arrange 2 Friendship Star units and 2 of the 3½″ × 3½″ string squares. Join the units into rows, pressing the seams toward the string units. Join the rows to complete a unit. Make 72.

BLUE TRIANGLE UNITS

Ⓕ Match a neutral and a blue 2⅞″ half-square triangle and stitch them together. Press the seam toward the blue. Remove the dog-ears and trim to 2½″ × 2½″ if needed. Make 216. Each of the 9 blocks will need 24 of these half-square triangle units. The units will measure 2½″ × 2½″ and finish at 2″ × 2″ in the quilt.

Ⓖ Arrange 3 of the blue and neutral half-square triangle units, filling in the diagonal of the pieced triangle with 3 blue half-square triangles. Join the units into rows, pressing the seams in opposing directions to encourage nesting of the seams. Join the rows. Make 72 pieced triangles.

Ⓗ Join a string triangle to a blue and neutral pieced triangle. Press the seams toward the blue triangles. Make 72. The units will measure 6½″ × 6½″ and finish at 6″ × 6″ in the quilt.

BLOCK ASSEMBLY

Ⓘ Arrange 2 blue triangle units with 2 stars and strings units. Join the units into rows, pressing the seams toward the blue triangles. Join the rows to complete quarter-block. Make 36. The units will measure 12½″ × 12½″ and finish at 12″ × 12″ in the quilt.

Ⓙ Arrange 4 quarter-blocks. Join them into rows, pressing the seams in opposing directions to facilitate nested seams. Join the rows to complete the block. Make 9. The blocks will measure 24½″ × 24½″ and finish at 24″ × 24″ in the quilt.

Sashing Construction

K Join 11 neutral 1½″ × 2½″ rectangles end to end. Press. Add a red half-square triangle unit to each end. Press the seams toward the neutral rectangles. Make 24. The sashing will measure 1½″ × 24½″.

Pieced Inner Border Units

L Join 5 neutral 1½″ × 4½″ strips end to end. Press. Add a neutral 1½″ × 1½″ square and a red 1½″ × 1½″ square to both ends. Press the seams toward the red squares. Make 12. The units will measure 1½″ × 24½″.

Quilt Assembly

Lay out blocks in 3 rows of 3 blocks each. Arrange the sashings and neutral cornerstones. Join the units into rows, pressing the seams toward the sashing and away from the cornerstones to facilitate seam nesting when joining the rows. Join the rows to complete the quilt center. Press.

ADDING BORDERS

Arrange the pieced inner border units around the quilt, using the remaining neutral 1½″ × 1½″ squares, red half-square triangles, and red 1½″ × 1½″ squares as spacers between the border lengths to complete the overlapping star design at the edges and corners of the quilt top. Join the units to complete borders.

Add the side borders to the quilt, pressing the seams toward the borders you just added.

Add the top and bottom pieced inner border to the quilt. Press the seams toward the borders you just added.

FLOATING BORDER

Join the 9 neutral 1½″ × width of fabric strips end to end, using diagonal seams to make a border length approximately 320″ long. Press the seams open.

Lay out the quilt center on the floor, smoothing it gently. Do not tug or pull. Measure the quilt through the center from top to bottom. Cut the side inner borders this length. Sew the side borders to the quilt, right sides together, pinning to match centers and ends easing where necessary to fit. Press the seams toward the borders you just added.

Repeat for the top and bottom borders, measuring across the quilt center, including the borders you just added in the measurement. Cut the top and bottom borders this length. Stitch the top and bottom borders to the quilt center, pinning to match centers and ends, easing where necessary to fit. Press the seams toward the borders you just added.

PIECED OUTER BORDER

M As with neutral string triangles (Step B), cover a 4½″ × 4½″ foundation square with blue fabric strips and strings. Make 84. Trim the units to 4½″ × 4½″. Cut the units on the diagonal across the strings to yield 168 string triangles. Carefully remove the paper.

N Place a red 1½″ × 6½″ strip and a blue string triangle right sides together, centering the long edge of the triangle on the edge of the strip. Stitch with a ¼″ seam. Press the seam toward the red strip. Add a string triangle to the opposite side. Press toward the red strip. Trim the unit to 4½″ × 4½″. Make 84.

O Join 20 string border units, turning them to complete a zigzag with the red centers. Make 4 borders.

Add a border to both sides of the quilt, pinning to match centers and ends and easing where necessary to fit. Press the seams toward the inner border.

P Add a string border unit to each end of the remaining 2 borders, continuing the zigzag pattern.

Add the top and bottom borders to the quilt, pinning to match centers and ends, easing where necessary to fit. Press the seams toward the inner borders.

Staystitch around the edge of the quilt by machine, using a long straight stitch, to keep the seams from popping open and to minimize stretch when quilting.

Finishing

Dawn's Early Light was machine quilted with light gray thread, using an edge-to-edge design called Star Spangled by Jessica Schick. A blue print binding finishes the quilt.

AT A GLANCE

A

String square
3½″ × 3½″ unfinished
Make 144.

B

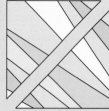

String triangles
6⅞″ × 6⅞″ unfinished
Make 72.

C

Red and neutral half-
square triangle unit
Make 640.

D

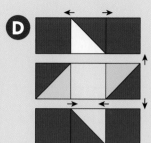

Friendship Star
3½″ × 3½″ unfinished
Make 144.

E

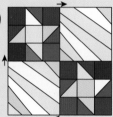

Stars and strings unit
Make 72.

F

**Blue and neutral half-
square triangle unit**
2½″ × 2½″ unfinished
Make 216.

G

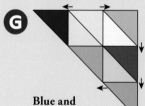

**Blue and
neutral pieced
triangle**
Make 72.

H

Blue triangle unit
6½″ × 6½″ unfinished
Make 72.

I

Quarter-block
12½″ × 12½″ unfinished
Make 36.

J

Big star block
24½″ × 24½″ unfinished
Make 9.

K

Sashing unit
Make 24.

L

Pieced inner border unit
Make 12.

String border unit
4½″ × 4½″ unfinished
Make 168 triangles.

Red strip insertion
4½″ × 4½″ unfinished
Make 84.

String borders
Make 4.

Top and bottom string borders
Make 2.

Quilt assembly

Crumb Jumble

FINISHED BLOCK: 6½″ × 6½″ · FINISHED QUILT: 72″ × 84″

MATERIALS

Assorted colored strips, strings, and scraps: 5 yards for blocks and border

Black-on-white print: 3 yards for block sashing and border

Blue solid: 3 yards for setting triangles and squares and spacer strips

Brown/blue stripe: ¾ yard for binding

Backing: 5¼ yards

Batting: 80″ × 92″

CUTTING

This quilt was designed to use small treasured scraps of fabric. There are no two blocks alike in this quilt and no specific cutting directions for the block centers. For construction methods, refer to Crumb Piecing Basics (page 14).

Assorted colored fabrics:

Cut 224 squares 1½″ × 1½″ for cornerstones.

Cut 284 squares 2½″ × 2½″ for border units.

Cut 4 squares 2⅞″ × 2⅞″ for border corners.

Black-on-white print:

Cut 224 strips 1½″ × 5″ for block sashing.

Cut 144 rectangles 2½″ × 4½″ for border units.

Cut 2 squares 2⅞″ × 2⅞″ for border corners.

Blue solid:

Cut 4 strips 1¾″ × width of fabric for top and bottom spacer strips. (See Trimming the Quilt Center, page 54.)

Cut 42 squares 7″ × 7″ for setting squares.

Cut 7 squares 10½″ × 10½″; subcut each square on the diagonal twice to yield 28 side triangles—26 will be used in the quilt and 2 will be extra.

Cut 2 squares 5½″ × 5½″; subcut each square on the diagonal once to yield 4 corner triangles.

Brown/blue stripe:

Cut 9 strips 2″ × width of fabric.

> **NOTE:** The letters in the following instructions refer to the letters on the illustrations in this project's At a Glance (pages 56 and 57).

WHAT CAN YOU DO WITH LEFTOVER STRIPS, STRINGS, HUNKS, CHUNKS, AND BONUS UNITS left from other projects? Stitch them all together in random fashion, making blocks big enough to trim to whatever size your heart desires! Sash the blocks, adding colorful cornerstones and a beautiful blue background, and create a striking on-point setting and a dynamic border and you are good to go.

I've always been a fly-by-the-seat-of-my-pants kind of quilter. I admit freely that I often don't know what borders are going to end up on any project until I get there. And sometimes that means that I've got to fudge and fuss with the math to get the idea in my head to fit the quilt. I quilt the way our grandmothers did. Mathematical imperfection has never stopped me from designing and making things work. Such is the case with the border on my version of this quilt.

But never fear! The instructions will give you a border that *will* fit without struggle for great results. Are you ready to dig in?

Block Construction

Ⓐ Referring to Crumb Piecing Basics (page 14), construct 56 blocks from scraps, strips, strings, and leftover units from previous projects. Join random fabric pieces in a stitch-and-flip manner, pressing and trimming after each seam, until a large enough section is created to cut to size.

Twist and turn the ruler before trimming to find the most interesting viewpoint. Trim the unit to 5″ × 5″. Make 56. The units will finish at 4½″ × 4½″ in the block.

Ⓑ Surround the center unit with 4 sashings 1½″ × 5″ and 4 cornerstones 1½″ × 1½″.

Join the units into rows, pressing the seams toward the sashing and away from the cornerstones.

Stitch the rows together to complete each block, pressing last 2 seams toward the outer edge of the block. Make 56. The blocks will measure 7″ × 7″ and finish at 6½″ × 6½″ in the quilt.

Quilt Center Assembly

Crumb Jumble is an on-point setting and is assembled in diagonal rows. Piecing diagonally set quilts into 2 halves keeps things from being too unwieldy when sewing a large quilt top.

Referring to the quilt assembly diagram, lay out the blocks and blue 7″ × 7″ squares, filling in the sides with the setting triangles and corner triangles.

Join the blocks and squares, setting triangles, and corner triangles into diagonal rows. Press the seams toward the blue squares and triangles. Join the rows into 2 quilt top halves.

Join the quilt top halves to complete the quilt center.

Trimming the Quilt Center

Build It Up!

Please note that depending upon your own seam allowance, the spacer border width we add to the top and bottom of the quilt may need to be adjusted. The unfinished measurement of the center after adding the two spacer borders is what matters so the pieced borders will fit. The width of border you need to add may vary depending upon your own sewing.

Measure the quilt from side to side across the center. It should be close to 64½″. If you are over that measurement, trim the long sides of the quilt equally on both sides to give you this measurement. There is a bit extra given in the size of the setting triangles to enable this.

Once the quilt measures 64½″ across the center, measure the quilt from top to bottom. You should have a measurement close to 74″. We need to bring the quilt length up to 76½″ by adding spacer strips top and bottom.

Join 2 blue 1¾″ × width of fabric strips end to end with a diagonal seam for the top spacer strip. Trim the seam, leaving a ¼″ seam allowance. Press the seam open. Repeat with the remaining 2 strips for the bottom spacer strip.

Trim both strips to 64½″ and sew to the top and bottom of the quilt center. Press the seams toward the strips just added.

The quilt center should now measure 64½″ × 76½″. Trim the top and bottom spacers equally to achieve this measurement if necessary.

Remember that pieced borders are stretchy, and we can accommodate a bit of difference easily over the length of the border.

Pieced Border

PIECED BORDER UNITS

C Draw a diagonal line on the wrong side of 284 assorted 2½″ × 2½″ squares—280 squares will be used for the double-diamond units and 4 squares for the border corner units.

Place a colored square on the right end of a black-on-white print 2½″ × 4½″ base rectangle, right sides together. Stitch just to the seam allowance side of the drawn line. Open and press the seam toward the triangle. Make 70.

Perfect Piecing

The drawn diagonal line in the stitch-and-flip technique is the fold line, not the stitching line!

Stitch right next to the drawn line with the stitching just into the seam allowance. The drawn line will end up on top of the thread when pressed, allowing the triangle to reach all the way to the edge of the base rectangle. Trim the excess fabric ¼″ away from the seamline. Press the seam toward the triangle you just added.

D In the same way, add another square to each of the border unit A rectangles. Trim the excess seam allowance and press the seam toward the *base rectangle*, not toward the triangle you just added. The seams on the back of unit should be pointing the same direction. Make 70.

E Repeat the process to make 70 border unit B rectangles, reversing the pressing directions. Press the right side triangle seams toward the base rectangles. Press the left side triangle seams toward the triangle.

F Join the units in pairs, pressing the center seams to one side. Make 34 A units and 34 B units. The units will measure 4½″ × 4½″ unfinished and finish at 4″ × 4″ in the quilt.

G Join unit A and unit B, aligning them so the seams will nest when stitching. Press the seam to one side. Make 2.

Cutting Tip

To cut the half-square triangle units in this step, I used 2½″ strips and the 2″ finished red line on my fast2cut Essential Triangle Tool (page 8).

H Place 2 colored and 2 black-on-white 2⅞″ × 2⅞″ squares right sides together. Cut on the diagonal once to yield 4 matched pairs of triangles ready to sew.

Pair 4 colored 2⅞″ × 2⅞″ squares right sides together. Cut on the diagonal once to yield 4 matched pairs of triangles ready to sew.

Stitch all 8 triangle pairs. Press the seams toward the colored triangles. Remove the dog-ears. The units should measure 2½″ × 2½″ and finish at 2″ × 2″ in the block.

Referring to the angle in the diagram, use the stitch-and-flip method to add just 1 corner square to the right side of the 4 remaining base rectangles. Trim the excess ¼″ beyond the seam and press the seams toward the triangles added.

I Lay out the units, join the 2 top triangle squares together into a row, and join the rows to complete the corner unit. Make 4. The units should measure 4½″ × 4½″ and finish at 4″ × 4″ in the quilt.

BORDER ASSEMBLY

J Join 9 double-diamond A units side by side. Press. Make 2.

Join 9 double-diamond B units side by side. Press. Make 2.

Stitch a border center C unit in between the A length and the B length. Press. Make 2.

Sew 1 border to each quilt side, pinning to match centers and ends and easing where necessary to fit. Press the seams toward the quilt center.

K Join 8 double-diamond A units side by side. Press. Make 2.

Join 8 double-diamond B units side by side. Press. Make 2.

Stitch an A length to a B length. Press. Make 2.

Add a border corner D unit to each end of the borders, paying attention to the direction that the corners turn. Press the seams toward the borders, away from the corner units.

Sew the top and bottom borders to the quilt, pinning and easing where necessary to fit. Press the seams toward the quilt center.

Finishing

Crumb Jumble was machine quilted in blue thread, using an edge-to-edge design called Entangled by Jodi Beamish of Gali Design. A brown/blue stripe became the perfect binding to finish the job.

AT A GLANCE

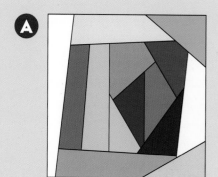

A

Crumb block center
5″ × 5″ unfinished
Make 56.

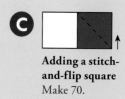

B

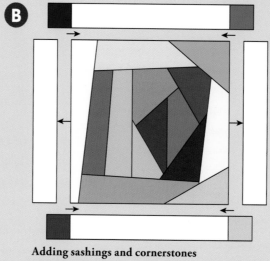

Adding sashings and cornerstones
7″ × 7″ unfinished
Make 56.

C

Adding a stitch-and-flip square
Make 70.

D

Repeat on opposite corner.
Make 70.

E

Border unit B
Make 70.

F

Double-diamond units A and B
4½″ × 4½″ unfinished
Make 34 of each.

G

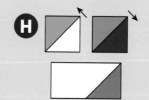

Border center unit C
Make 2.

H

Border corner unit D assembly

I

Border corner unit D

J

Border assembly

K

Top and bottom border assembly

Quilt assembly

Xing!

FINISHED BLOCK: 6″ × 6″ • FINISHED QUILT: 73½″ × 82¾″

MATERIALS

Foundation paper: 49 sheets 8½″ × 11″. Cut 15 squares 7¼″ × 7¼″, 4 squares 4¼″ × 4¼″, and 224 squares 3½″ × 3½″.

Assorted colored scraps and strings: 8 yards for blocks and setting triangles

Assorted neutral scraps: 2 yards for blocks

Aqua solid: 1¾ yards for sashing

Red print 1: ¼ yard for cornerstones

Red print 2: ¾ yard for binding

Backing: 7 yards

Batting: 82″ × 91″

CUTTING

Star Blocks

Cutting is for 1 star block. Cut a total of 72 sets of patches

This quilt was designed to use small treasured scraps of fabric. There are no two blocks alike in this quilt and no specific cutting directions for the center unit. For construction methods to make a crumb-pieced 3⅜″ × 3⅜″ center square, refer to Crumb Piecing Basics (page 14).

> *Cutting Tip*
>
> *I used 1½″ fabric strips and the 2″ finished green line on my fast2cut Essential Triangle Tool to cut the quarter-square triangles in the star blocks. Traditional rotary cutting instructions are given for those who don't have this ruler. (Refer to Quarter-Square Triangles, page 9.)*

Colored scraps:

Cut 2 matching squares 3¼″ × 3¼″; subcut each square on the diagonal twice to yield 8 star points.

Neutral scraps:

Cut 1 matching set of 4 squares 2½″ × 2½″ and 1 square 3¼″ × 3¼″; subcut square on the diagonal twice to yield 4 background triangles.

String Blocks

Cut a variety of light, medium, and dark scraps into random widths from ¾″ to 2″ for string pieced blocks and setting triangles. Cut enough to get going; cut more variety as needed.

Sashing

The sashing pieces on each end of the "sashing and cornerstone" rows are cut longer than the sashings between the blocks, and the extra length takes the place of half-cornerstones at the edge of the quilt, as they are small enough to be lost in the binding.

Aqua solid:

Cut 258 strips 1″ × 6½″ for block rows.

Cut 30 strips 1″ × 7″ for ends of sashing rows.

Cornerstones

Red print 1:

Cut 127 squares 1″ × 1″.

Binding

Red print 2:

Cut 9 strips 2″ × width of fabric.

> **NOTE:** The letters in the following instructions refer to the letters on the illustrations in this project's At a Glance (pages 62 and 63).

XING IS THE CHINESE WORD FOR *STAR*. The shapes and configurations of stars within patchwork are many and oh, so varied! Stars are also a favorite of many, and I am right there in their midst. I love a scrappy star design.

The stars in *Xing!* started out their life as a way to use up many small crumb blocks I had made and left lying forgotten in a bag in the depths of a sewing room cupboard. Using them as star centers was the easy part. Setting the blocks after they were made became the challenge.

Small string blocks became the alternate block creating interesting secondary designs, and the narrow aqua solid sashing used up leftovers from *Daybreak* (page 72).

Those tiny red pin dot cornerstones? There really *is* a place to use up 1990s fabrics. Proof that if you cut it small enough, it's not ugly!

Block Construction

STAR BLOCKS

A Referring to Crumb Piecing Basics (page 14), construct 72 block centers from scraps, strips, strings, and leftover units from previous projects. Join random fabric pieces in a stitch-and-flip manner, pressing and trimming after each seam until a large enough section is created to cut to size.

Twist and turn the ruler before trimming to find the most interesting viewpoint. Trim unit to 3⅜″ × 3⅜″. Make 72.

B Add a colored star point triangle to 2 adjoining sides of a background corner square. Press the seams toward the star point triangles. Trim the dog-ears. Make 2.

C Referring to the diagram, stitch 4 pairs of star point and background triangles in mirror image—2 with the star point on the right, and 2 with the star point on the left. Stitch pairs to the 2 remaining 2½″ × 2½″ background squares, pressing the seams toward the triangles. Trim the dog-ears. Press. Make 2.

D Add the star point A units to opposite sides of crumb-pieced center square. Press the seams away from the center square.

Add star point B units to the 2 remaining sides. Trim the dog-ears. Press.

E The blocks should measure 6½″ × 6½″ and finish at 6″ × 6″ in the quilt. Make 72.

STRING BLOCKS

F Referring to String Piecing Basics (page 11), cover the 3½″ × 3½″ paper foundations in a stitch-and-flip manner, pressing and trimming after each seam until foundation square are covered. Trim the blocks to 3½″ × 3½″. Carefully remove the paper. Make 224.

G Join 4 string block units in an X formation. Stitch the units into rows, pressing the center seams in opposing directions to nest. Join the rows. Press. Make 56. The blocks will measure 6½″ × 6½″ and finish at 6″ × 6″ in the quilt.

STRING SETTING TRIANGLES

H Cover the 7¼″ × 7¼″ paper foundations in a stitch-and-flip manner, pressing and trimming after each seam until a large enough section is created to cut to size. Trim the blocks to 7¼″ × 7¼″. Cut each block on the diagonal once to yield 30 setting triangles. Carefully remove the paper.

STRING CORNER TRIANGLES

I Cover the 4¼″ × 4¼″ paper foundations in a stitch-and-flip manner, pressing and trimming after each seam until a large enough section is created to cut to size. Trim blocks to 4¼″ × 4¼″. Cut each block on the diagonal once to yield 8 corner triangles. Carefully remove the paper. Stitch 2 triangles together to form a string corner. Press. Make 4.

Quilt Assembly

Xing is an on-point setting and is assembled in diagonal rows. Rows of blocks separated by sashings alternate with rows of sashings and cornerstones.

Lay out the blocks, setting triangles, sashings, and cornerstones as shown in the quilt assembly diagram (page 63). The longer 7″ sashings are attached to each end of the sashing and cornerstone rows only. The longer ends will overlap the sashings at each end of the block rows, with the excess being trimmed after assembly. There are no cornerstones at the edge of the quilt.

Join the units into rows, pressing the seams toward the sashings and away from cornerstones. Join the rows to complete the quilt top. Press.

I like to piece a diagonally set quilt in 2 halves. This keeps things from being too unwieldy, especially when sewing a large quilt top. Join the quilt top halves to complete the quilt.

Square up the edges of the quilt, leaving ¼″ seam allowance beyond the corners of the star blocks. Much like a front porch lattice, the sashings do not end in a point and will be blunted when the binding is applied.

Finishing

Xing was machine quilted in pale aqua thread, using an edge-to-edge design called Gossamer by Hermione Agee of Lorien Quilting of Australia. I love the red print binding that finishes the edge—it's got crow's feet! (And so do I!)

AT A GLANCE

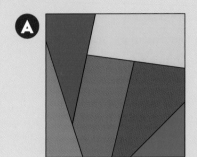

A

Star block center
3⅜″ × 3⅜″ unfinished
Make 72.

B

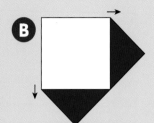

Star point unit A
Make 2.

C

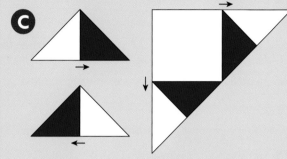

Star point unit B
Make 2.

D

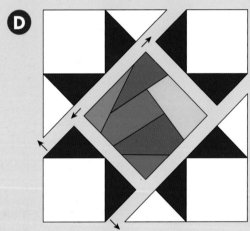

Star assembly

E

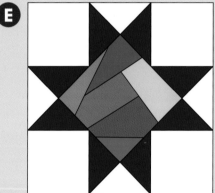

Completed star block
6½″ × 6½″ unfinished
Make 72.

F

String block unit
3½″ × 3½″ unfinished
Make 224.

G

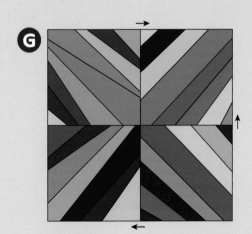

String block
6½″ × 6½″ unfinished
Make 56.

H

String setting triangles
7¼″ × 7¼″ unfinished
Make 30 triangles.

I

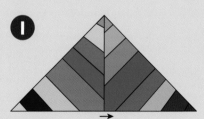

String corner triangle
Make 4.

Quilt assembly

Emerald City

FINISHED BLOCK: 24″ × 24″ • FINISHED QUILT: 84″ × 84″

MATERIALS

Foundation paper: 63 sheets 8½″ × 11″. Cut 90 squares 5½″ × 5½″ and 36 squares 5″ × 5″.

Assorted green scraps and strings: 7 yards

Assorted neutral scraps and strings: 8 yards

Bright green print: ¾ yard for binding

Backing: 8 yards

Batting: 92″ × 92″

CUTTING

Half-Square Triangles

> *Cutting Tip*
>
> *To cut the many needed half-square triangles in this quilt, I used 2″ strips and the red 1½″ finished line on my fast2cut Essential Triangle Tool (page 8). It is so much easier to cut from 2″ strips than to cut from 2⅜″ × 2⅜″ squares. And pairs of triangles are cut with right sides already together and ready to sew.*

Green fabrics:

Cut 504 squares 2⅜″ × 2⅜″; subcut each square on the diagonal once to yield 1,008 half-square triangles.

Neutral fabrics:

Cut 558 squares 2⅜″ × 2⅜″; subcut each square on the diagonal once to yield 1,116 half-square triangles.

String Blocks and Triangles

Cut neutral and green scraps into random widths from ¾″ to 2″ for string piecing the block units. Short strips can be used by joining them end to end to create the needed length to reach across the paper foundation and add more interest to the blocks. Cut enough to get going; cut more variety as needed.

Block Centers

Green fabrics:

Cut 36 squares 2″ × 2″.

Sashing and Cornerstones

Green fabrics:

Cut 168 rectangles 1½″ × 2½″.

Cut 128 squares 1½″ × 1½″.

Neutral fabrics:

Cut 384 strips 1½″ × 3½″.

Cut 256 squares 1½″ × 1½″.

Binding

Bright green print:

Cut 9 strips 2″ × width of fabric.

> **NOTE:** The letters in the following instructions refer to the letters on the illustrations in this project's At a Glance (pages 68–71).

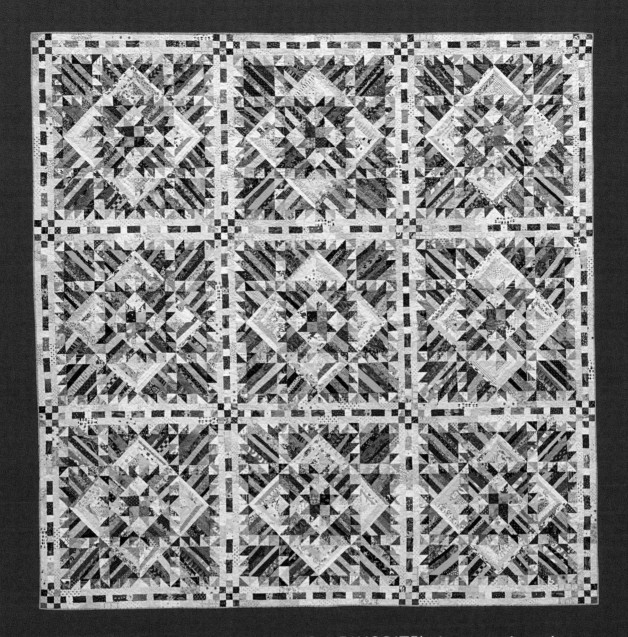

TWO-COLOR QUILTS ARE ALWAYS A FAVORITE! I love two-color quilts.

When playing with numerous scraps and strings by color family, the array of tones and shades is joyous with so much interest. No two string blocks are the same and there is always something new to see when playing with color and value. When choosing fabrics for this quilt, push your boundaries in all directions with fabrics ranging from light to dark within each color. The greens in *Emerald City* run from very yellow green to a dark blue green and everywhere in between.

There are many, many pieces in this quilt, but only nine 24″ blocks total and the extra piecing is worth it! Instead of making all the half-square triangle units at once, you can work them in batches, or cut several sets ahead of time (I used my fast2cut Essential Triangle Tool and 2″ strips for the triangles in this quilt), and use the matched pairs of triangles as "leaders and enders" in between the string block piecing. (For more information, see my books *Adventures with Leaders & Enders* and *More Adventures with Leaders and Enders*, available from C&T Publishing.)

Block Construction

STRING UNITS

(A) Referring to String Piecing Basics (page 11), cover 5″ × 5″ square paper foundations with green strips in a stitch-and-flip manner, pressing and trimming after each seam until the foundation squares are covered. Make 36. Trim the units to 5″ × 5″. Carefully remove the paper. The units will finish at 4½″ × 4½″ in the quilt.

(B) Cover 5½″ × 5½″ paper foundations with green strips in a stitch-and flip-manner, pressing and trimming after each seam until the foundation squares are covered. Make 54. Trim the units to 5⅜″ × 5⅜″.

Cut each unit on the diagonal once across the strings to yield 108 green string triangles. Carefully remove the paper.

Go Wider!

Because the neutral string squares are cut down the middle of the center strings, it helps to place a wider string of about 2″ corner to corner across the foundation, adding narrower strings on either side to fill the foundation. Don't go too narrow with the center strip!

(C) Cover 5½″ × 5½″ paper foundations with neutral strips in a stitch-and-flip manner, pressing and trimming after each seam until the foundation squares are covered. Make 36. Trim the units to 5⅜″ × 5⅜″.

Cut each unit on the diagonal once down the center string to yield 72 neutral string triangles. Carefully remove the paper.

(D) Join a green string triangle to a neutral string triangle, using a ¼″ seam. Press the seam toward the neutral triangles. Trim the string blocks to 5″ × 5″. The units will finish at 4½″ × 4½″ in the quilt. Make 72.

HALF-SQUARE TRIANGLE UNITS

(E) Match a neutral half-square triangle with a green half-square triangle and stitch them together. Press the seam toward the green. Remove the dog-ears and trim to 2″ × 2″ if needed. Make 1,008. Each of the 9 blocks will need 112 of these half-square triangle units. The units will measure 2″ × 2″ and finish at 1½″ × 1½″ in the quilt.

(F) Join 3 half-square triangle units to make triangle strip A. Press the seams toward the green triangles. Make 144. The units will measure 2″ × 5″.

(G) Join 4 half-square triangle units to make triangle strip B. Press the seams toward the neutral triangles. Make 144. The units will measure 2″ × 6½″.

STAR CENTER UNITS

H Lay out 2 half-square triangle units, 1 green 2″ × 2″ square, and 3 neutral half-square triangles. Assemble the units into rows and join the rows to complete the star center triangle. Press. Make 36.

I Join a green string triangle to a star center triangle. Press the seam toward the green triangle. Make 36. The units will measure 5″ × 5″ and finish at 4½″ × 4½″ in the quilt.

ADD TRIANGLE STRIPS

J Referring to the diagram, first add a triangle strip A to the right side of star center unit. Press the seam toward the green triangle. Complete unit by adding triangle strip B. Press the seam away from the green string triangle and toward the small triangles. Make 36. The units will measure 6½″ × 6½″ and finish at 6″ × 6″ in the quilt.

K Add triangle strip A to the right side of a green and neutral string unit, pressing the seam toward the green string triangle. Add triangle strip B to the adjoining green side, pressing the seam toward the small triangles. Make 72. The units will measure 6½″ × 6½″ and finish at 6″ × 6″ in the quilt.

L Add triangle strip A to the right side of a green string unit, pressing the seam toward the green string unit. Add triangle strip B to the adjoining side, paying attention to the direction the strings are facing. Press the seam toward the small triangles. Make 36. The units will measure 6½″ × 6½″ and finish at 6″ × 6″ in the quilt.

BIG BLOCK ASSEMBLY

M Arrange 4 green string units, 4 star center units, and 8 green/neutral string triangle units to complete the block layout. Join the units into rows, pressing the seams in opposing directions to facilitate nesting when the rows are joined. Join the rows to complete the block. Press. The blocks will measure 24½″ × 24½″ and finish at 24″ × 24″ in the quilt. Make 9.

Sashing Construction

N Join 8 neutral 1½″ × 3½″ strips end to end to create one length 1½″ × 24½″. Press the seams in one direction. Make 48.

O Alternate 8 neutral 1½″ × 1½″ squares with 7 green 1½″ × 2½″ rectangles. Add a green 1½″ × 1½″ square to each end to complete center sashing. Press the seams toward the green squares. Make 24.

P Join the edge sashings to either side of a center sashing. Press the seams toward the edge sashings. Make 24 pieced sashing strips.

Q Lay out green and neutral 1½″ × 1½″ squares in nine-patch format. Join the squares into rows, pressing the seams toward the neutral squares. Join the rows to complete nine-patch. Press the row seams toward the block center. Make 16.

Quilt Assembly

Lay out blocks in 3 rows of 3 blocks each. Arrange the sashings and cornerstones as shown in the quilt assembly diagram (page 71). Join the units into rows, pressing the seams toward the sashing and away from the cornerstones to facilitate seam nesting when joining the rows. Join the rows to complete the quilt top. Press.

Finishing

Emerald City was machine quilted using sand-colored thread in an edge-to-edge design called Pinwheel #4 by Patricia E. Ritter of Urban Elementz. A bright green binding with a ¼″ finish cut from 2″ strips finishes the edge.

AT A GLANCE

Green string square
5″ × 5″ unfinished
Make 36.

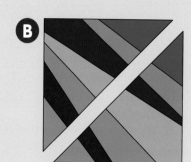

Green string triangles
5⅜″ × 5⅜″ unfinished
Make 108 triangles.

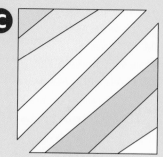

Neutral string triangles
5⅜″ × 5⅜″ unfinished
Make 72 triangles.

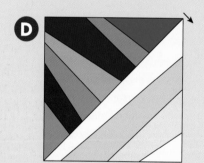

Joining string triangles
5″ × 5″ unfinished
Make 72.

Half-square triangle unit
2″ × 2″ unfinished
Make 1,008.

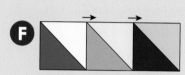

Triangle strip A
2″ × 5″ unfinished
Make 144.

Triangle strip B
2″ × 6½″ unfinished
Make 144.

H

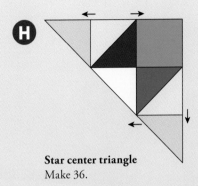

Star center triangle
Make 36.

I

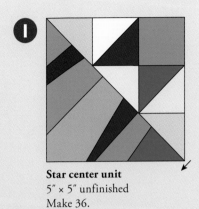

Star center unit
5″ × 5″ unfinished
Make 36.

J

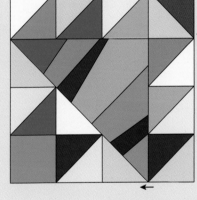

Add triangle strips to star center unit.
6½″ × 6½″ unfinished
Make 36.

K

Add triangle strips to string triangle unit.
6½″ × 6½″ unfinished
Make 72.

L

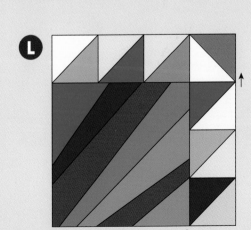

Add triangle strips to green string square.
6½″ × 6½″ unfinished
Make 36.

Block construction
24½″ × 24½″ unfinished
Make 9.

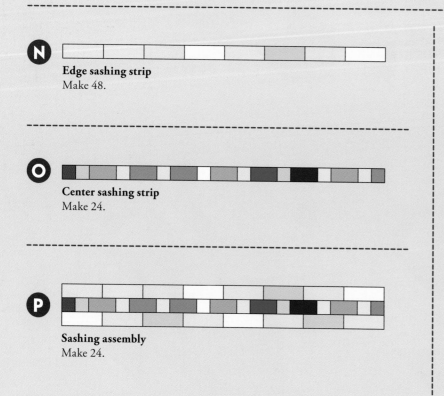

N **Edge sashing strip**
Make 48.

O **Center sashing strip**
Make 24.

P **Sashing assembly**
Make 24.

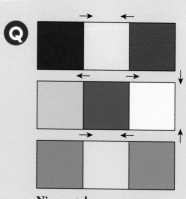

Q **Nine-patch cornerstone**
Make 16.

Quilt assembly

Daybreak

FINISHED BLOCK: 8″ × 8″ · FINISHED QUILT: 73″ × 83″

MATERIALS

Foundation paper: 43 sheets 8½″ × 11″

Assorted neutral scraps: 6 yards for blocks, string sashing, and outer border

Assorted colored scraps: 3 yards for blocks and cornerstones

Aqua solid: 2¼ yards for blocks, cornerstones, and inner border

Mocha print: ¾ yard for binding

Backing: 7 yards

Batting: 81″ × 91″

CUTTING

Four-Patches

The small sparkling four-patches in this quilt were the perfect place to use up a box of random 1½″ strips that were taking over my stash. As scraps vary in length, no exact number of strips to cut is given. What matters is the number of units you can get out of the strip sets you have sewn. Cut, sew, and cut some more as needed until you have reached the number of subcuts required for the 210 four-patches in the blocks, plus the 56 cornerstones.

Neutral fabrics:

Cut several 1½″ strips.

Colored fabrics:

Cut several 1½″ strips.

Aqua solid:

Cut 5 strips 1½″ × width of fabric.

On-Point Triangles

Colored fabrics:

Cut 168 matching pairs of 2 squares 2½″ × 2½″; subcut pairs of squares on the diagonal once to yield 4 corner triangles for each four-patch.

Neutral fabrics:

Cut 42 matching pairs of 2 squares 2½″ × 2½″; subcut pairs of squares on the diagonal once to yield 4 corner triangles for each four-patch.

Block Backgrounds and Inner Border

Aqua solid:

Cut 84 squares 2⅞″ × 2⅞″; subcut each square on the diagonal once to yield 168 half-square corner triangles.

Cut 42 squares 5¼″ × 5¼″; subcut each square on the diagonal twice to yield 168 side triangles.

Cut 8 strips 1½″ × width of fabric for inner border.

Cutting Tip

To cut the half-square corner triangles from 2½″ strips, I used the 2″ finished red line on my fast2cut Essential Triangle Tool (page 8). I also used the 4″ finished green line on the tool to cut the quarter-square side triangles from 2½″ strips. (Refer to Quarter-Square Triangles, page 9.)

String Sashings and Outer Border

Neutral fabrics:

Cut into random widths from ¾″ to 2″ for string pieced sashings and border. Strips should measure at least 10″ long, though shorter strips can be joined end to end to create the needed length. Cut enough to get going; cut more variety as needed.

Binding

Mocha print:

Cut 9 strips 2″ × width of fabric.

NOTE: The letters in the following instructions refer to the letters on the illustrations in this project's At a Glance (pages 76 and 77).

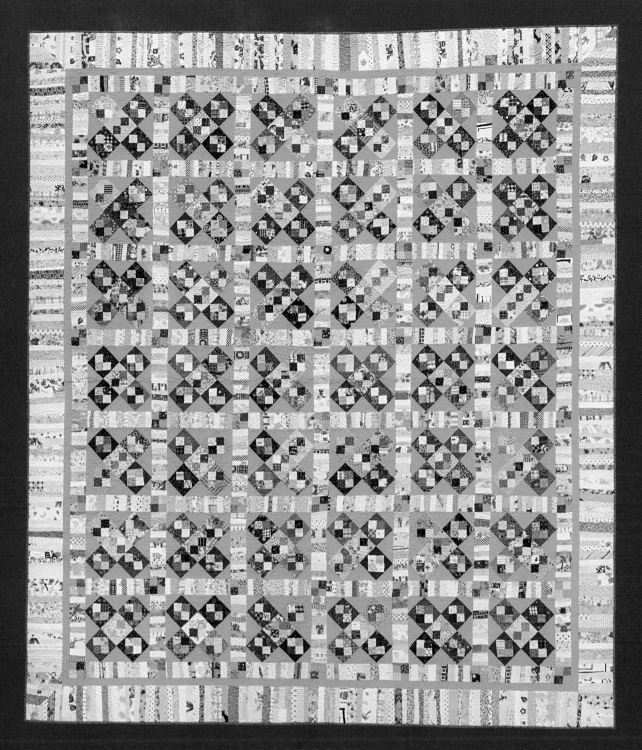

DAYBREAK IS MY FAVORITE TIME OF DAY. I am a morning person. I love the promise of the new day ahead, my choice as to how I'm going to fill it up and make good use of it. Will I quilt today? I hope so!

This quilt has extra special meaning to me as the aqua fabric in the blocks and inner border was inherited from my mother-in-law who passed away on Christmas morning, 1983. It took until 2016 for me to finally use it.

This quilt brings the peace of the new day ahead to my heart as I remember so fondly the woman who gave life to my husband.

Block Construction

BLOCK FOUR-PATCHES

A Match 1½″ neutral strips with 1½″ colored strips in random fashion, sewing for as much variety as possible within the four-patch units. I find that working with short strips helps increase variety in strip sets. Press the seams toward the darker strips and measure. The strip sets should measure 2½″ wide at this point. Adjust the seam allowance if the proper width is not reached. Make several strip sets to get going, and make more as needed to achieve the number of four-patches required.

Place 2 different strip sets right sides together with the seams opposing, preparing to cut matched pairs of units ready to sew.

Crosscut each matched strip set into 1½″-wide segments. Each cut will yield a four-patch pair ready to sew. Keep sewing and cutting strip sets, as needed, until you have 210 matched four-patch sets.

B Sew each pair together to make a four-patch. Press. The units will measure 2½″ × 2½″ and finish at 2″ × 2″ in the block.

ADDING TRIANGLES

Cutting Hint

I find it helpful to make the corner triangles a bit larger and then square my unit to size after adding them. The size of these triangles has been increased just a bit to allow for trimming.

C Center and stitch 2 matching triangles on opposite sides of a four-patch. Press. Trim the dog-ears even with the sides of the four-patch.

Add 2 remaining matching triangles. Press. Make 168 units with colored corners and 42 with neutral corners. Each block requires 4 units with colored corners and a center unit with neutral corners.

D Trim the units, leaving ¼″ seam allowance beyond the four-patch corners. The units will measure 3¼″ × 3¼″.

BLOCK ASSEMBLY

E Lay out the block units, placing 4 units with colored corners around the center unit with neutral corners. Fill in the block background with aqua side and corner triangles.

This block is assembled in diagonal rows. Join the units into rows, and then join rows to complete the block. Make 42. The blocks will measure 8½″ × 8½″ and finish at 8″ × 8″ in the quilt.

The Fudge Factor

Are blocks not coming out the size they should? It's no problem! Just measure the average size of the blocks and cut the sashing to this length.

Sashing Construction

CORNERSTONES

F Refer to Block Four-Patches (at left) to make four-patches, using an assortment of 1½″ colored strips paired with aqua strips. Make 56. The units will measure 2½″ × 2½″ and finish at 2″ × 2″ in the quilt.

STRING SASHINGS

G Referring to String Piecing Basics (page 11), cover 8½″ × 11″ sheets of foundation paper with neutral strings in a stitch-and-flip manner, pressing and trimming after each seam until the paper foundations are covered. Make 25.

Trim the excess fabric beyond the paper. Cut 4 sashing strips 2½″ × 8½″ across the width of the paper. Repeat to make 97 sashings 2½″ × 8½″. Remove the paper.

String Borders and Corners

H In the same manner, cover 18 sheets of foundation paper with neutral strings. Cut 2 border units 5″ × 8½″ from each. Carefully remove the paper.

Join the border units end to end into one length, approximately 288″. Press.

Corner Tip

Though the quilt looks like it has mitered corners, it doesn't! I used my fast2cut Essential Triangle Tool (page 8) to cut these corner triangles in matched pairs with right sides together all ready to sew. Add a few strips to the 5″ × 10″ piece of border left over to make it at least 12″ long. Cut into 2 pieces 5″ × 6″. Place both 6″ lengths of 5″ string border with right sides together. Using the 4½″ finished red line on the tool, cut 4 triangle pairs ready to sew. Stitch. Press. The corner units will measure 5″ × 5″, the same size as the border width.

I If you are not using a fast2cut Essential Triangle Tool (page 8), string piece to cover 4 foundation paper 6″ × 6″. Trim squares to 6″ × 6″ and carefully remove the paper. Place 2 squares right sides together, with strips facing the same direction and cut on the diagonal once to yield 2 triangle pairs ready to sew. Repeat with the remaining 2 squares. Stitch the triangle pairs. Press. Trim the 4 corner blocks to 5″ × 5″.

Quilt Assembly

Lay out the blocks, sashings, and cornerstones as shown in the quilt assembly diagram (page 77), paying attention to the placement of the aqua squares in the cornerstones.

Join the units into rows, pressing the seams toward the blocks and cornerstones. Join the rows to complete the quilt center. Press.

INNER BORDER

Join the 8 aqua border strips end to end using diagonal seams to make a border length approximately 318″. Trim and press the seams open.

Lay out the quilt center on the floor, smoothing it gently. Do not tug or pull. Measure the quilt through the center from top to bottom. Cut the side inner borders this length. Sew the side borders to the quilt sides, right sides together, pinning to match the centers and ends and easing where necessary to fit. Press the seams toward the borders.

Repeat for the top and bottom borders, measuring across the quilt center, including the borders you just added in the measurement. Cut the top and bottom borders this length. Stitch the top and bottom inner borders to the quilt center, pinning to match the centers and ends and easing where necessary to fit. Press the seams toward borders.

OUTER BORDER

Referring to Inner Border (above), measure the quilt from top to bottom, and cut 2 side string borders this length. Next, measure the quilt from side to side, and cut 2 top and bottom string borders this length.

Sew the side borders to the quilt sides, right sides together, pinning to match centers and ends and easing where necessary to fit. Press the seams toward the inner borders.

Add the border corner units to each end of the top and bottom borders, pressing the seams toward the corner units. Stitch the top and bottom borders to the quilt, pinning to match the centers and ends and easing where necessary to fit. Press the seams toward the borders.

Staystitch around the edge of the quilt by machine, using a long straight stitch, to keep the seams from popping open and to minimize stretch when quilting.

Finishing

Daybreak was machine quilted with aqua thread, using an edge-to-edge design called Marmalade by Patricia E. Ritter and Leisha Farnsworth. A mocha print binding brings a touch of warmth to the edge of the quilt.

AT A GLANCE

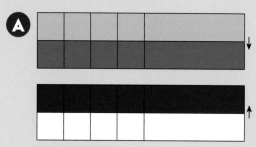

Four-patch strip set

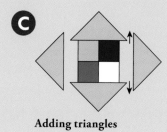

Four-patch
2½″ × 2½″ unfinished
Make 210.

Adding triangles

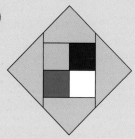 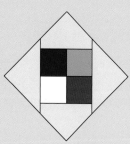

Make 168.   Make 42.

Trimming and squaring

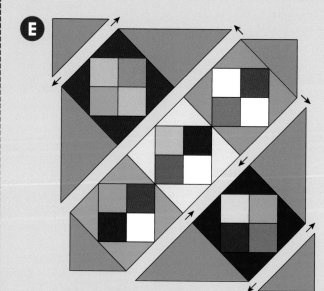

Block assembly
8½″ × 8½″ unfinished
Make 42.

**Cornerstone four-patch
strip set and assembly**
2½″ × 2½″ unfinished
Make 56.

G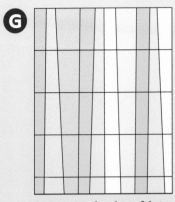

String pieced sashing fabric
Make 25.

H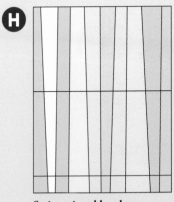

String pieced borders
Make 18.

I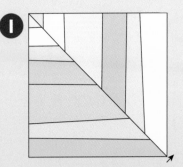

String pieced corners
5″ × 5″ unfinished
Make 4.

Quilt assembly

Punkin' Patch

FINISHED BLOCK: 6″ × 8″ • FINISHED QUILT: 56″ × 70″

MATERIALS

Foundation paper: 49 rectangles 4½″ × 6½″. (Try Carol Doak's Foundation Paper by C&T Publishing. You can get 2 rectangles out of an 8½″ × 11″ sheet.) Also make a copy of border unit foundation patterns (page 93).

Assorted orange scraps: 3 yards for blocks and border

Assorted gray scraps: 4 yards for blocks and border

Assorted green scraps: 1¼ yards for blocks and border

Orange stripe: ⅝ yard for binding

Backing: 3¾ yards

Batting: 64″ × 78″

CUTTING

Orange scraps:

Cut random widths from ¾″ to 2″ for string pieced pumpkins. Strips should measure at least 5″ long, but shorter strips can be joined end to end to create the needed length. Cut enough to get going; cut more variety as needed.

Cutting Tip

To cut the half-square triangles for the outer border of this quilt, I used 2½″ strips of the gray and orange scraps and the 2″ finished line on my fast2cut Essential Triangle Tool (page 8). I also used the 4″ green line on the tool to cut the quarter-square triangles (page 9). Traditional rotary cutting measurements are given for those who don't have access to this ruler.

Cut 15 squares 5¼″ × 5¼″; subcut each square on the diagonal twice to yield 60 quarter-square base triangles for Flying Geese border.

Cut 2 squares 2⅞″ × 2⅞″; subcut each square on the diagonal once to yield 4 border corner triangles.

Gray scraps:

Cut 12 assorted strips 1″ × width of fabric or the equivalent in shorter scraps for borders 1 and 3.

Cut 18 assorted strips 1½″ × width of fabric or the equivalent in shorter scraps for checkerboard border.

Cut 60 squares 2⅞″ × 2⅞″; subcut squares on the diagonal once to yield 120 half-square wing triangles for Flying Geese border and border corners.

Cut 49 matched sets of 2 rectangles 2½″ × 3″, 1 strip 2½″ × 6½″, and 4 squares 1¾″ × 1¾″.

Green scraps:

Cut 18 assorted strips 1½″ × width of fabric or the equivalent in shorter scraps for checkerboard border.

Cut 49 rectangles 1½″ × 2½″ for stems.

Orange stripe:

Cut 7 strips 2″ × width of fabric.

> **NOTE:** The letters in the following instructions refer to the letters on the illustrations in this project's At a Glance (pages 82 and 83).

WITH THE ARRIVAL OF AUTUMN COME THE THOUGHTS, COLORS, AND FLAVORS OF THE SEASON—pumpkins in all their varieties! I have fond memories of going out to the local pumpkin patch with my brothers as a young child, and running through the rows, looking for just the right one—the one that would be the "best one ever!"

Just thinking about it also recalls the memorable aroma of candles burning brightly through the smiling faces of happy jack-o'-lanterns bidding their welcome greeting on my front door step each Halloween night.

The rows of scrappy pumpkins, some up and some down in placement remind me of those days running up and down the rows in the "punkin' patch" of my childhood.

Block Construction

PUMPKIN BASES

A The pumpkins are created by covering 4½″ × 6½″ rectangles of foundation paper with narrow strips of orange fabrics. Referring to String Piecing Basics (page 11), cover the 49 foundation rectangles in a stitch-and-flip manner, pressing and trimming after each seam. Trim to 4½″ × 6½″. Remove the paper.

B Draw a diagonal line from corner to corner on the wrong side of 4 matching 1¾″ × 1¾″ squares. Place the squares on the corners of the base unit, right sides together.

The drawn lines are the pressing lines. Stitch *right next to* the line toward the corner you will be trimming. The line will end up on top of the thread when pressed and the triangle will be able to fold all the way over to reach the edges of the pumpkin base. Stitch all 4 corners in this manner. Trim the seam allowance ¼″ from the stitching line. Press the seams toward the triangle corners.

Make 49.

IMPROV STEMS

C Use a green 1½″ × 2½″ stem rectangle and a gray scrap to create each pumpkin stem with its own angle. All are different—no two stems are alike!

Place the gray scrap on the stem piece, right sides together, at a pleasing angle. Stitch ¼″ from the edge of the gray scrap.

Press the seam toward the gray scrap, making sure the gray completely covers the upper portion of the green rectangle underneath.

Turn the unit over and trim the excess gray beyond the green rectangle. Trim the seam allowance to ¼″. The units will measure 1½″ × 2½″ and finish at 1″ × 2″ in the completed block. Make 49.

BLOCK ASSEMBLY

D Lay out the pumpkin units. Stitch 2½″ × 3″ background rectangles to either side of the stem unit. Press the seams toward the rectangles.

Join the stem unit to the top of the pumpkin. Press the seam toward the stem unit.

Add a 2½″ × 6½″ background strip to the top of 28 pumpkin blocks and press the seams toward the stem units. Add background strips to the bottom of the remaining 21 pumpkin blocks. Press the seams toward the background strip. The blocks will measure 6½″ × 8½″ and finish at 6″ × 8″ in the quilt.

Checkerboard Border

As scrap strips vary in length and shorter strips provide more variety, don't focus on the number of strips sets you need to make; focus on the number of subcuts required to build the border. You will need enough strip sets to make 216 units.

E Stitch green 1½″ strips to gray 1½″ strips, pressing the seams toward the gray. Join 2 pairs of strips together, alternating gray with green, into panels 4 strips wide. Press toward the gray.

Crosscut the strip sets into 1½″ sections. Cut 216.

F Join 57 units together for the side checkerboard border. Press. Make 2

Join 51 units together for the top/bottom checkerboard border. Press. Make 2.

Flying Geese Border

G Stitch a gray wing triangle to the right side of an orange base triangle, pressing the seam toward the orange triangle.

Add a matching left gray wing triangle to the unit, pressing the seam allowance toward the gray. Pressing this way will permit the seams to nest easily when sewing them end to end into the border lengths. Remove the dog-ears. The units should measure 2½″ × 4½″ and finish at 2″ × 4″ in the border. Make 58.

CENTER SIDE UNIT

H Paper piece the border unit foundations in numerical order, pressing and trimming after each patch addition. Make 2 units with orange centers and matching gray side triangles, 1 for each side border. The units will measure 2½″ × 2½″ and finish at 2″ × 2″ in the quilt.

BORDER CORNER UNIT

I Join orange and gray 2⅞″ half-square corner triangles, right sides together. Press the seam toward the gray. Trim the dog-ears. Make 4. The units should measure 2½″ and finish at 2″ in the border.

FLYING GEESE BORDER ASSEMBLY

J Join 8 Flying Geese units. Press. Make 4.

Stitch a border unit in between 2 Flying Geese sections to complete 1 side border. Press. Make 2.

K Join 13 Flying Geese units. Press. Add a half-square triangle corner unit to both ends of the border length. Press the seams toward the corner triangle units. Make 2.

Quilt Assembly

Referring to the quilt assembly diagram (page 83), lay out the pumpkin blocks in rows as desired, alternating "down" pumpkins with "up" pumpkins.

Join the blocks into rows, pressing the seams in an alternate fashion to facilitate nested seams as rows are joined.

Join the rows to complete quilt center. Press.

PIECING BORDERS 1 AND 3

Join random lengths of gray 1″ strips end to end to create a length approximately 440″ long.

From this length:
- Cut 2 strips 1″ × 56½″ for border 1 sides.
- Cut 2 strips 1″ × 43½″ for border 1 top and bottom.
- Cut 2 strips 1″ × 65½″ for border 3 sides.
- Cut 2 strips 1″ × 52½″ for border 3 top and bottom.

BORDER ASSEMBLY

Sew the border 1 side borders to the quilt sides, right sides together, pinning to match centers and ends and easing where necessary to fit. Press the seams toward the borders.

In the same way, stitch the border 1 top and bottom strips to the quilt center. Press the seams toward the borders.

Stitch the side checkerboard borders to the sides of the quilt; press the seams toward border 1.

Add the top and bottom checkerboard borders to the quilt; press the seams toward border 1.

Add the border 3 strips in the same way as border 1. Press the seams toward the strips you just added.

Add the Flying Geese side borders to the quilt, pinning to match centers and ends and easing where necessary to fit. Press the seams toward border 3.

Add the Flying Geese top and bottom borders to the quilt in the same manner, pressing the seams toward border 3.

Staystitch around the edge of the quilt by machine, using a long straight stitch, to keep the seams from popping open and to minimize stretch when quilting.

Finishing

Punkin' Patch was machine quilted with light gray thread, using an edge-to-edge design called Hall of Mirrors by Apricot Moon Designs. What better fabric for binding this quilt could there be than an orange stripe!

AT A GLANCE

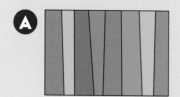

A

String pumpkin base
4½″ × 6½″ unfinished
Make 49.

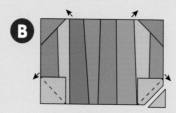

B

Adding corners
Make 49.

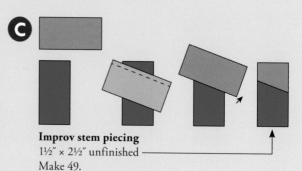

C

Improv stem piecing
1½″ × 2½″ unfinished
Make 49.

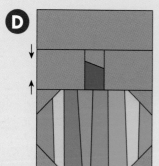 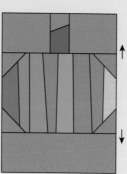

Make 28. Make 21.

Pumpkin block assembly
6½″ × 8½″ unfinished

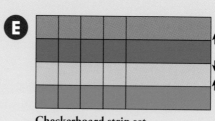

E

Checkerboard strip set
Cut 216 segments.

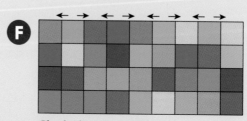

F

Checkerboard assembly

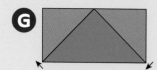

G

Flying Geese
2½″ × 4½″ unfinished
Make 58.

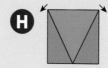

H

Border unit
2½″ × 2½″ unfinished
Make 2.

I

Half-square corner unit
2½″ × 2½″ unfinished
Make 4.

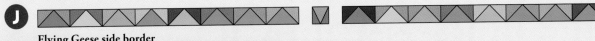

J

Flying Geese side border
Make 4.

K

Flying Geese top and bottom border
Make 2.

Quilt assembly

Indigo-a-Go-Go

FINISHED BLOCK: 4½″ × 4½″ • FINISHED QUILT: 78½″ × 87½″

MATERIALS

Foundation paper: 81 sheets 8½″ × 11″. Cut 127 squares 5″ × 5″, 64 rectangles 3″ × 5″, and 4 squares 3″ × 3″.

Assorted neutral scraps: 8½ yards for blocks and border

Assorted indigo scraps: 2¼ yards for blocks and border

Cheddar solid: 1¾ yards for blocks

Neutral print: ¾ yard for binding

Backing: 7¼ yards

Batting: 86″ × 95″

CUTTING

As scraps vary in width and length, no exact number of strips to cut is given. What matters is the number of units you can get out of the strip sets you have sewn for the nine-patches, or the strips required to do the string pieced block units. Cut, sew, and cut some more as needed until you have reached the number of units required.

Neutral scraps:

Cut several 2″ strips for blocks.

Cut strips in random widths from ¾″ to 2″ for blocks and inner border. Strips should measure at least 5½″ long, though shorter strips can be joined end to end to create the needed length. Cut enough to get going; cut more variety as needed.

Cut 212 squares 2⅜″ × 2⅜″; subcut each square on the diagonal once to yield 424 half-square corner triangles.

Indigo scraps:

Cut several 2″ strips for blocks.

Cut 106 squares 2⅝″ × 2⅝″ for border.

Cheddar solid:

Cut 576 squares 2″ × 2″.

Neutral print:

Cut 9 strips 2″ × width of fabric.

Cutting Tip

To cut the half-square corner triangles for the square-in-a-square border units, I used 2″ neutral strips and the 1½″ finished red line on my fast2cut Essential Triangle Tool (page 8).

NOTE: The letters in the following instructions refer to the letters on the illustrations in this project's At a Glance (pages 88 and 89).

I'M SURE I'M NOT THE ONLY QUILTER WHO HAS STARTED
A PROJECT, SET THE PROJECT ASIDE, AND FORGOT
ABOUT THE PROJECT until it resurfaces years later while in pursuit of
something completely and totally unrelated. What? You haven't done that?
When it happens to you all you will be able to do is laugh at yourself, give
up on whatever the original idea was, and go with the flow for something
new. That's exactly what happened to me with these nine-patches. More
than 200 of them.

They were made with South African fabrics I had been collecting for a
number of years, also known as Shweshwe. Wax-resist dyed, they must be
prewashed to remove excess dye and sizing. I love working with them.

If working with Shweshwe, please note that the fabric is narrower than our
traditional 40"-wide yardage and more yardage is required.

The cheddar solid fabric is a staple in my stash, and I love how it adds just

Nine-Patch Blocks

A Sew indigo 2″ strips on each side of a neutral 2″ strip to make strip set A. Press the seams toward the indigo strips. To get as much variety as possible, sew short strip sets and mix up the fabrics. Crosscut the strip sets into 2″-wide segments. Cut a total of 256 segments.

Sew 3 neutral strips together in the same manner to make strip set B. Press the seams toward the center strip. Make several and crosscut the strip sets into 2″-wide segments. Cut a total of 128 segments.

B Sew a segment A on either side of a segment B to make a nine-patch. Press the seams toward the indigo. Make 128. The blocks will measure 5″ × 5″ and finish at 4½″ × 4½″ in the quilt.

String Snowball Blocks

C The string squares are created by covering 5″ × 5″ squares of foundation paper with narrow strips of neutral fabric. Referring to String Piecing Basics (page 11), cover the 127 paper foundations in a stitch-and-flip manner, pressing and trimming after each seam. Trim to 5″ × 5″ and carefully remove the paper.

D Draw a line from corner to corner on the wrong side of 4 cheddar 2″ × 2″ squares. Place a marked square on the corner of a string square, right sides together. Stitch with the needle kissing up to the drawn line just within the seam allowance. Trim excess fabric ¼″ from the stitching. Press the seam toward the triangle. Repeat with the 3 remaining squares to complete 1 string snowball block. Make 127.

Stitch-and-Flip Success!

Do not sew on the line! The line is the fold line, not the stitching line. Set the needle just to the right of the line, toward the outer corner of the unit. This way the line will fold up and end up directly on top of the thread where it belongs, and the edge of the stitch-and-flip corner will reach the unit's outer edges.

String Rectangles

Half-blocks with and without corner triangles complete the design around the center of the quilt, before the outer border is added.

E Follow the same procedure to make string rectangles as with string squares, using the 3″ × 5″ foundation rectangles. Trim the units to 3″ × 5″. Make 64.

Set aside 30 string rectangles to be used as spacers. The remaining 34 string rectangles will have stitch-and-flip corners added.

F Using the stitch-and-flip method (see Stitch-and-Flip Success!, below left), add 2 cheddar corners to each of the remaining string rectangles. Trim the excess fabric from behind each corner, leaving a ¼″ seam allowance. Make 34.

String Corner Blocks

G Place a center strip from corner to corner over a 3″ × 3″ foundation square with right side up. Add strips to either side of the center strip until the paper base is completely covered. Press. Trim the unit to 3″ × 3″ and carefully remove the paper. Make 4.

Quilt Assembly

Referring to the quilt assembly diagram (page 89), lay out the blocks in rows, alternating the nine-patch blocks with the string snowball blocks and using the string rectangles and corner units around the outside edge of the center to complete the design. Pay attention to the direction that the strings in the string snowball blocks run; they alternate every row.

Join the units into rows, pressing the seams toward the nine-patch blocks to enable the seams to nest when rows are joined. Join the rows to complete the quilt center. Press.

SQUARE-IN-A-SQUARE BORDER

H Stitch neutral 2⅜″ half-square triangles to opposite sides of an indigo 2⅝″ × 2⅝″ square. Press the seams toward the square. Add triangles to the remaining 2 sides of the square. Press toward the triangles. Remove the dog-ears. The seams will nest as units are joined in the border. The units will measure 3½″ × 3½″ and finish at 3″ × 3″ in the quilt. Make 106.

I Join 27 units side by side, with seams nesting, to complete the side border. Press. Make 2.

Sew the side borders to the quilt sides, right sides together, pinning to match the centers and ends and easing where necessary to fit. Press the seams toward the borders.

J Join 26 units together in the same manner to make top/bottom border. Press. Make 2. Add the top and bottom borders to the quilt, right sides together, pinning to match centers and ends and easing where necessary to fit. Press the seams toward the borders.

Staystitch around the edge of the quilt by machine, using a long straight stitch, to keep the seams from popping open and to minimize stretch when quilting.

Finishing

Indigo-a-Go-Go was machine quilted with sand-colored thread, using an edge to edge design called Country Garden by Hermione Agee of Lorien Quilting of Australia. Wanting those blue squares to float at the edge of the quilt, I applied a neutral binding, using 2″ strips for a ¼″ binding finish.

On the Reverse!

Being short on the backing fabric that I wanted, I used *more* blocks to piece a panel to extend the backing fabric from the realm of "not enough" to "just right"! It always makes me feel good to be able to shop my stash and make it work.

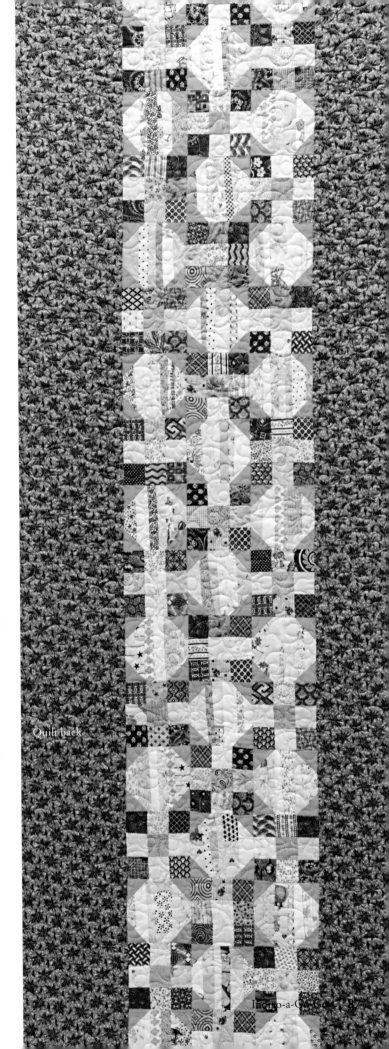

Quilt back

AT A GLANCE

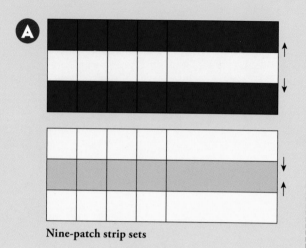

A

Nine-patch strip sets

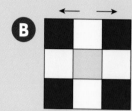

B

Nine-patch
5″ × 5″ unfinished
Make 128.

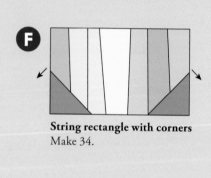

C

String square
5″ × 5″ unfinished
Make 127.

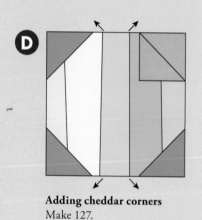

D

Adding cheddar corners
Make 127.

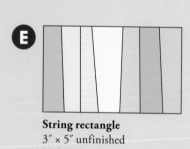

E

String rectangle
3″ × 5″ unfinished
Make 64.

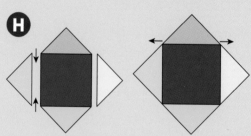

F

String rectangle with corners
Make 34.

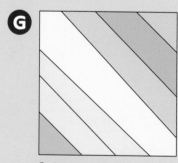

G

String corner unit
Make 4.

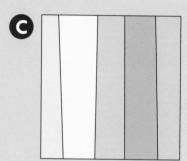

H

Square-in-a-square border unit
3½″ × 3½″ unfinished
Make 106.

I

Square-in-a-square side borders
Make 2.

J

Top and bottom borders
Make 2.

Quilt assembly

Patterns

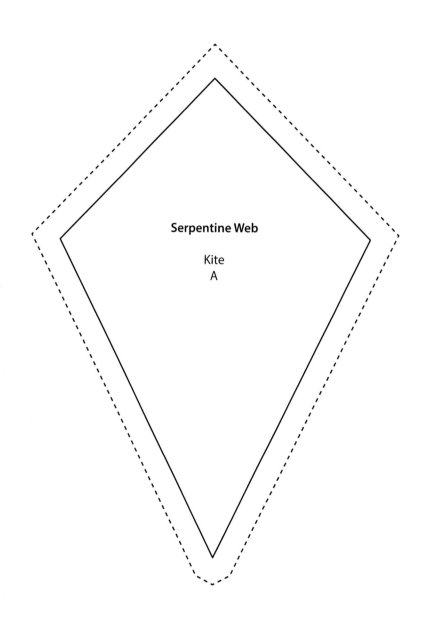

Serpentine Web

Kite
A

Make 72 copies of this page to get 144 of the Star Point foundation pattern.

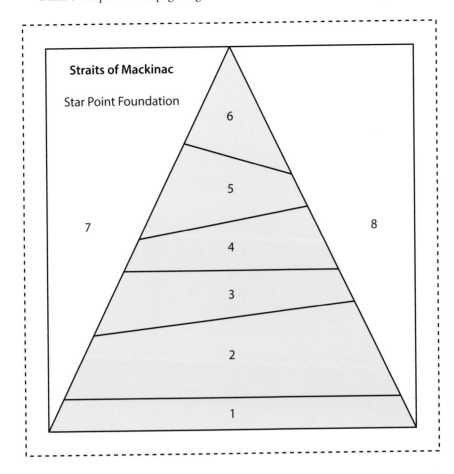

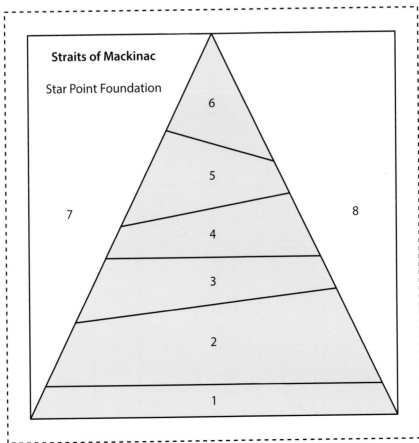

Make 45 copies of this page to get 540 of the Sashing and Border Unit foundation pattern.

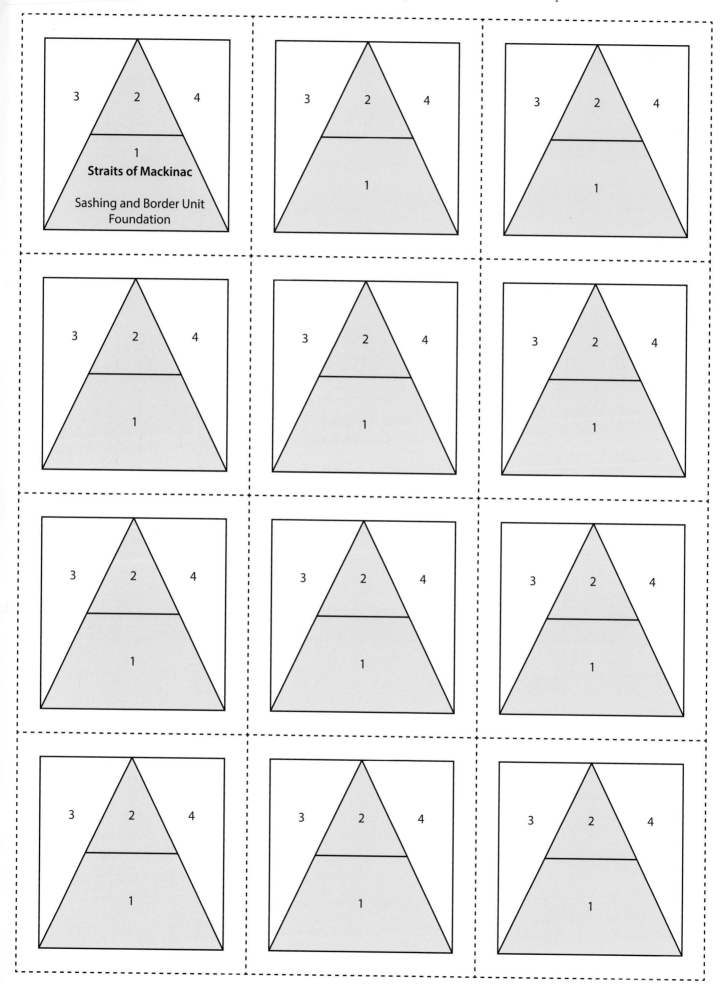

Make 1 copy of this page to get 2 of the Border foundation pattern.

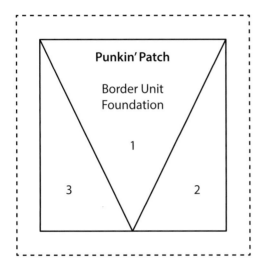

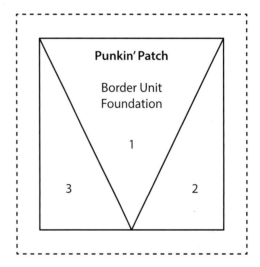

About the Author

BONNIE K. HUNTER is passionate about quiltmaking, focusing mainly on scrap quilts with the simple feeling of "making do." She began her love affair with quilting in a home economics class during her senior year of high school in 1980 and has never looked back.

Dedicated to continuing the traditions of quilting, Bonnie enjoys meeting with quilters, teaching workshops, and lecturing to quilt guilds worldwide—challenging quilters to break the rules, think outside the box, and find what brings them joy.

When not on the road, you can find Bonnie stitching away at her mountain cabin in her beloved corner of the Blue Ridge mountains of Southwest Virginia, dreaming up new designs, always captivated by the ever-present thought of "What if?!"

Bonnie's favorite motto? "The Best Things in Life Are Quilted!", *of course!*

Visit Bonnie online!

Website: quiltville.com

Facebook: /quiltvillefriends

Instagram: @quiltville_bonnie

Also by Bonnie K. Hunter:

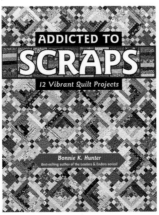

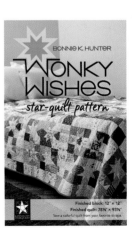

Want even more creative content?

Make it, snap it, share it
using
#ctpublishing

31901064122585